For Judy and Ian

Disclaimer

The material in this publication is of the nature of general comment only, and does not represent professional advice. It is not intended to provide specific guidance for particular circumstances and it should not be relied on as the basis for any decision to take action or not take action on any matter which it covers. Readers should obtain professional advice where appropriate, before making any such decision. To the maximum extent permitted by law, the author and publisher disclaim all responsibility and liability to any person, arising directly or indirectly from any person taking or not taking action based on the information in this publication.

connecting
profit with
purpose

How to create a
world-changing business

PHIL PRESTON

'The role of business in society is radically changing. Commitment to a social purpose is becoming a competitive advantage, and corporate leaders who want to master this approach need to read this book. Preston sets out a clear, actionable and persuasive approach to creating shared value, filled with examples of companies of all sizes and from all parts of the world, that have created meaningful social change in ways that have also created success for their companies and themselves. Whether you are a senior executive or just starting out in business, you will benefit from Preston's guidance and experience.'

Mark R. Kramer, Co-Founder & Managing Director of FSG and Senior Lecturer at Harvard Business School

contents

introduction

Two years after *Fortune Magazine* launched its Change the World List[1], a little-known company featured at number 13. This small but growing Australian regional bank looked out of place because it was surrounded by global giants like Apple, Walmart, Toyota and Unilever. In terms of size it ranks about 75th on our local stock exchange. Its name is Bendigo and Adelaide Bank. Why is it there? What did it do to earn 13th place on this global list? Topping the list in that same year was JP Morgan Chase & Co. Large banks aren't usually front of mind when we're asked to name the best social contributors, so what did it do to gain this accolade? On the other side of the world a Danish bioscience company called Chr. Hansen was crowned the world's most sustainable company[2]. What did it do to achieve this level of recognition and how does that add to its bottom line?

In this book we're going to unpack the methods that these and other leading companies are using to link profitable business with social purpose. Instead of seeing societal challenges purely as risks to manage, they embrace them as sources of innovation, pushing their thinking and strategies beyond the boundaries that we're accustomed to. Philanthropic support and corporate social responsibility programmes have long been in place – but have they made a difference? They have in some areas but, in the main, they are designed

1

to create positive perceptions of businesses and have insufficient resources behind them to solve the underlying problems. They are more about preserving corporate brand and reputation, and protecting their licence to operate in the community. We will be looking at how leading companies have added a new layer to their management skill set and devised more inclusive and intelligent ways of making and sustaining their profits.

Why is this important? In most developed countries the corporate sector is many times larger than the government and not-for-profit sectors. The potential is tantalising: to find a commercially sound way of utilising private sector resources to solve pressing challenges. Given the persistent bad press about corporate greed and wrongdoing, that may sound like an impossible task. However, I'll contend that it is possible to grow profits while doing good. The question we will be addressing is this: what principles and methods are these leading companies using, how can we codify that process and how can we replicate it many times over?

When you're working in or with a large business, making a difference is hard work. You may volunteer or donate to social and environmental causes either through workplace programmes or in your own time – although finding enough time outside of work to participate can be challenging. You may feel good about what you do, but still think that it seems small-scale or token compared to the number and magnitude of the issues on this planet that need addressing. You may feel frustrated or conflicted because there are things going on in your business that are causing harm to someone or something. Growth targets or cost-cutting goals put pressure on even the best people to do things that are less than perfect. Calling out those practices can be a career-limiting move, and anyway it's hard changing entrenched behaviours without total buy-in and commitment from the top. The scope of this book and its methods are not limited to one or two corporate roles: they are applicable to board members looking for something more, CEOs looking to get an edge or create an enduring legacy, company strategists looking for new ideas, managers and leaders who are seeking greater purpose from their work in a way that is congruent with profitability, leaders of people and culture worried about employee engagement, or millennials looking for a company that is authentic and powerful in its commitment to making a difference.

Before discovering the principles that are the subject of this book, I was working in a corporate role and thinking that I should try to earn big money so I could become rich, retire early and then make a difference by giving back. On one hand it was a noble pursuit, but on the other a little dispiriting to think that I might have to wait many years to be rich enough to give back. The only other option would have been to get a job with a not-for-profit organisation and do more purposeful work... which would also have meant a big reduction in salary and bonus potential. That wasn't something Karen and I were prepared to do when saddled with a mortgage and raising two young children. It's the sort of dilemma you or people you know may be facing. You may be resigned to the fact that your ability to change the world single-handedly will elude you for the foreseeable future. Worse still, the set of values you live by at home may be different to those you are forced to adopt during work hours. Ouch!

It wasn't until I'd transitioned from my corporate career and set up my own business that it became clear we can actually make a much bigger difference through our work than outside it. If you are feeling a bit jaded with your job or career, how would it be if you could help find new sources of profitability that also contribute to large-scale, positive social change? It is achievable, and the aim of this book is to provide the know-how for you to get started. In fact, you may already be applying the principles that we're talking about, and this will give you comfort that you're not on your own – that there is a formal management language to describe your mindset and methods. If you work for a small to medium-sized business, the same principles and techniques will work for you too, with the added benefit that you can act with more speed and autonomy to put your ideas into action.

Alternatively, if you work for a not-for-profit organisation the same principles will equip you with new ways for engaging businesses in deeper and more strategic conversations. And, if you have influence over government policy or processes, you'll learn how to play an enabling role so that companies and not-for-profits do more of the heavy lifting for you. Harnessing more private sector resources is the aim, and the only way to get real traction – to access those resources at scale – is to connect the outcomes you're seeking with corporate profitability. There are many companies out there who may be willing to help – you've just got to work out who they are, and how to approach them and develop solutions together.

A recurring theme in this book is that conventional approaches to making a difference are only playing at the edges. We'll be introducing a singular concept that brings business back to what it is designed to do: serve the genuine needs of customers and the communities it operates in. Best of all, if you can play a part in implementing these principles you'll gain greater satisfaction from your role and you'll be doing it all on work time! It's an approach that seamlessly combines social good with commercial smarts: one that sees purpose and profitability reinforcing each other. I can't think of when there's been a greater need, nor a better time, to make these principles and techniques more accessible. Critics of capitalism often proclaim that business should "do good" without providing alternatives that are realistic and achievable. Our approach is practical, workable and scalable.

We will take a closer look at companies connecting profit with purpose to see what's driving them. Along the way, we'll unpack the reasons why consumer brands like Nestlé have become more focused on their social purpose and why several real estate agents have been so keen to help to reduce tenancy evictions in their areas. We'll examine the pathway a medical products company followed to put billions of dollars of investment into safer injection systems and why leading insurers are proactively investing in preventative health, reducing car accident black-spots and working with governments to mitigate natural disaster impacts. The same principles are being used to help long-term unemployed and disadvantaged people gain access to entry-level roles in food processing and other blue collar industries. They've underpinned the rise of a low alcohol beer brand, the employment of senior citizens in parcel delivery challenges, and drastically reduced input costs for a farm operator. That's just a sample; there'll be many more that we will examine to find the common formula for doing world-changing business.

This book presents a far-reaching idea that is fit for the times, and backs it up with the critical thinking and methods that you'll need to put it into action. It's been formalised by experts in the business strategy, management and not-for-profit fields. Although the concept is always received positively, I've found that many people struggle to bridge the gap between enthusiasm and implementation. An idea is only powerful if it can be put into action, and the experiences I've had in applying and observing these principles for over a decade have led to the insights presented here. You don't need to be a billionaire or high-flying corporate executive to drive this; you can influence better ways of doing business whatever your position or role. The concept won't solve every single problem we face, but it does induce greater corporate investment in the challenges that affect us all.

The book is divided into four sections. Section I is about the tensions between business and society, questioning whether profit and purpose can fit together comfortably – or is capitalism so flawed that it will never work? We look at the methods companies and investors have already tried for doing good and why they haven't succeeded at scale. A shift in thinking is needed to create solutions, and there's good reason why purpose is moving from being a decorative corporate feature to one that drives profitability.

We'll then unpack the "shared value" concept in Section II, which provides a way forward for marrying profit with purpose. A raft of examples shows how leading companies are using it right now to create a performance or strategic edge. We then pause for a moment to differentiate shared value from philanthropy and corporate social responsibility programmes and appreciate the power it brings relative to those approaches. We round out the section by classifying different types of strategy and examining the role that government and not-for-profits can play in creating win-win outcomes.

Section III provides you with methods and processes you can use to generate and develop your own ideas. Having the right mindset is the main prerequisite – one that acknowledges that our fortunes are linked and therefore businesses can't expect to operate independently of society and succeed in the future. We'll look at five practical ways for getting started, along with extra tips that will help you get the most out of your endeavours. And finally, in Section IV, there's a chance to reflect on what it all means and the immediate actions you can take to change the world for the better.

If this sounds exciting, let's get going.

SECTION I
overcoming competing interests

WHEN businesses cause harm, the reper-
cussions are often felt far and wide
highlighting competing interests between
shareholders and society. Where there's profit
to gain, corporate behaviours can become less
than acceptable. Is this an intractable problem?
Is capitalism broken or have we just been using it
badly? In this section we'll explore these tensions
in more detail and why the methods that companies
have been using to be 'good' or 'responsible' hav-
en't really worked. It sets the scene for the shift in
mindset and behaviour that's needed if businesses
and society are to go hand in hand instead of head
to head.

chapter 1
increasing tensions

Wherever we look we find tensions between competing interests. In professional sports, athletes trade off ongoing hunger with strict dietary regimes aimed at optimising performance; during events they need to get the right balance between instantaneous effort and over-all endurance. How they manage their diet and food intake leading up to an event is important because the wrong strategy will impact their results. Likewise, good economics is about the efficient and effective use of resources, which leads to tensions when one group of people – say the shareholders of a company – exploit commonly owned resources for their own financial gain.

This may happen because the resources in question are underpriced, poorly regulated, poorly policed or all three, and it also means that companies may have little incentive to change their behaviour. The term *tragedy of the commons* was coined by British economist William Forster Lloyd to describe the tension between selfish uses of free resources and the common good. For example, consider a mining company polluting river water and undermining the health and live-lihoods of people located downstream: they may not care about the state of the water when it leaves their site because they've already used and profited from it. Or the makers of tobacco products that reap profits and leave behind a litany of public healthcare costs for taxpayers to bear; or clothing brands exploiting people economically trapped in unsafe, slave-like conditions.

Are there businesses with enough will and momentum to really change, or shall we be having this same discussion in perpetuity? There are forces at play elevating social purpose beyond a nice-to-have feature to becoming an essential part of the engine room of business.

Defy the trend at your peril

The global population has risen from around two billion people to nearly eight billion over the past 100 years. We are on track to reach 9.7 billion by 2050[3]. This means that we are pushing up against the ecological boundaries of our planet and things will only get worse in the foreseeable future. We are using up our natural resources at 1.75 times the rate they are replenished[4]. Demand for food is forecast to grow by 60 per cent from today's levels, raising the prospect of food security risks, hunger, poverty and nutritional challenges. The impact of greenhouse gas emissions on climate change, and rates of resource depletion and flora and fauna losses are out of control. Credible scientists[5] believe we've missed our chance to prevent climate change and should instead focus our efforts on adaptation to a much harsher future. If you were an alien life form looking down on the human race you'd be excused for thinking that we put profits ahead of planetary survival, whereas in fact the former won't be relevant without the latter. The first order risks are more important than the second order ones.

Our problems are wide and varied. World Economic Forum research points to pressures on water resources, agriculture, skills for digital and artificial intelligence related work, access to financial products and services, poverty, homelessness, healthcare, gender parity, inclusion and more. Many of these are intertwined, such as climate change, forest clearing, food production, food security and nutrition. Despite a 40 per cent lift in the UN Human Development Index over the past 40 years – reflecting rising health, income and education levels – there's still a lot of work to do. I could go on detailing our problems but, suffice to say, the take-away message is that all parts of our society have to work better together and evolve at a rapid rate to head off disastrous impacts[6].

Most, if not all, of the challenges we face will have flow-on effects to the bottom lines of businesses. For example, the three levels of government in Australia have jointly committed[7] to working with industry to ensure that all packaging will be reusable, recyclable or compostable by 2025. That's an ambitious goal considering it needs the support of local and global food brands, supermarket chains, more than 500 local government areas, packaging suppliers, waste carriers, recycling facilities, various not-for-profits and us, the consumer. There will be corporate winners and losers across the supply chain during this transition. Looking further afield, the insurance industry is exposed to rising claims from natural disasters and weather events. Research[8] points to rising sea levels, higher temperatures, stronger cyclones, drought, and bushfire risk. Australia has just experienced bushfire activity and property loss on an unprecedented scale and, while we can't directly attribute a single event like this to climate change, it is consistent with the modelling and forecasts made by scientists. As customers experience hefty premium increases and more assets become uninsurable, the fundamentals of the industry deteriorate. Global reinsurer Lloyd's of London warns[9] the industry is at a tipping point on climate change and is pushing companies to take action. In the food and grocery sector, an overabundance of sugar-laden foods has increased obesity and the incidence of diseases such as diabetes. As public healthcare costs rise, the companies making these products shouldn't count on sympathy from consumers, regulators or government. A tax on sugar content has already been mooted as a way of improving health and decreasing healthcare costs.

Defy these and other trends at your peril; they aren't going away any time soon. A leading group of proactive and forward-looking companies is finding ways to take advantage of these ingrained trends while others struggle to respond. The methods presented in this book provide a blueprint for you to join them if you have not already done so.

Relentless change

As well as prevailing ecological and social pressures, technological advances and digitisation are reducing the cost structures of many industries. The level of change and disruption is a cause of corporate restructuring. McKinsey & Co, a company we'll examine in a different light later on, has found[10] that most global corporations are in a permanent state of organisational flux. This also means that collaborative ways of working are increasingly attractive – partnerships, alliances and joint ventures, for example, help businesses bring new knowledge, skills and resources on board quickly and at a lower cost to buying them or building them from scratch. Experts in the public and private sectors note[11] that collaboration must be embraced as a guiding principle, more so than competition in our hyperconnected world. And CEOs regard collaborating across traditional organisational boundaries as a premium capability[12] because there is a growing demand for people who can work seamlessly with new types of partners and stakeholders. We'll be drawing on the value that can be realised through collaborations and partnerships as we explore the combination of profit and purpose.

12

Measuring progress

Our default way of measuring progress is very dollar-oriented and doesn't always reflect the real strength and vibrancy (or despair) of the places we live in. Gross Domestic Product (GDP) – the financial value of goods and services produced over a time period – is the main indicator economists focus on. We are conditioned to feel good if it is going up. That's fair enough in many respects because economic activity will generally correlate with employment rates, but it only tells one part of the overall story about the health of our society. It's possible for company profits or country GDP numbers to look strong now while also being unsustainable in the future because they've come at the cost of running down non-financial assets such as natural resources, living conditions, economic inclusion or public infrastructure. We can't keep taking from one side of the ledger and expecting the other side to hold up. We know these less visible assets contribute to our prosperity and resilience, but they can remain hidden from view. "If the GDP is up, why is America down?" Simon Kuznets, the economist who helped develop GDP, warned the US Congress back in 1934. To push home the point, Robert F. Kennedy made his own landmark observations[13] about the shortcomings of financial measures as a proxy for societal health:

"Yet the gross national product does not allow for the health of our children, the quality of their education or the joy of their play. It does not include the beauty of our poetry or the strength of our marriages, the intelligence of our public debate or the integrity of our public officials. It measures neither our wit nor our courage, neither our wisdom nor our learning, neither our compassion nor our devotion to our country, it measures everything in short, except that which makes life worthwhile."

An interesting way of analysing the non-financial health of countries has been developed by the Social Progress Imperative[14]. Its indices bring together a number of indicators such as nutrition levels, basic medical care, access to clean water, shelter, personal safety, information, health, wellness, environmental quality, personal freedoms and rights, inclusiveness, and access to education. Based on these measures, Australia, New Zealand, Japan, Canada, Sweden, Norway, Finland, France, Germany, the United Kingdom and a handful of other European countries are rated in the top tier. The US is in the next tier and there are six tiers in total. These indices highlight the areas that policy makers should focus on if they want to support a healthy and sustained level of economic growth.

When the headline numbers look good but non-financial assets are being undermined in creating them, that's a problem and it's often the lack of visibility between cause and effect that prevents us from taking decisive action. Some businesses have taken advantage of these less visible connections.

The trust deficit

Issues like the exploitation of labour and working conditions have a long history, from the East India Company's dreadful behaviour on the subcontinent to Carnegie's union-breaking practices in his own steel mills[15] through to Nike's Asian sweat shop sourcing practices in the 1990s. We've seen ecological disasters from Union Carbide's Bhopal gas leak in India resulting in more than 20,000 deaths to the Exxon Valdez oil spill and the unwanted proliferation of plastic waste. Alcohol abuse, tobacco products, gaming, sugary foods and many other products place a drain on the public purse because they contribute to social problems. These are examples of companies generating externalities – costs resulting from their actions that are imposed on others. Bear in mind that what they're doing is legal, technically and otherwise. Extracting or using fossil fuels is not against the law; however emissions are created when they are burned and increasing CO2 levels is an externality. There are very few meaningful financial penalties for digging up coal, extracting and refining oil, driving petrol-fuelled cars, flying planes, clearing forests and so on.

Because some externalities do create community concern or unfavourable press coverage, companies have become good at managing these risks either through investments designed to assuage their consciences or initiatives that try to minimise harm. The amount of good they do through these means can easily be dwarfed by the problems caused in their core business practices. To illustrate, the following[16] describes a multinational company that, at the time, had more than 8,000 employees volunteering in community projects and was donating millions to charitable causes:

> *"While focusing on children's health projects and educational programmes for underprivileged youth, the [foundation] also partners with cultural organisations that enrich the quality of life in our communities."*

On the surface this looks like a responsible and highly prestigious company to work for – one that would attract the best and brightest graduates who have a preference for working with companies that do good. Alas, the information pertains to Lehman Brothers… before it went into bankruptcy. They were heavily involved in creating and selling US sub-prime mortgage products (described afterwards as "toxic debt"), where loans of questionable quality were being pooled and then refinanced or on-sold to investors in global capital markets. When default rates on the underlying mortgage loans started rising, the value of most of these toxic products fell precipitously. Lehman Brothers itself got stuck with too many of these problem assets on its own balance sheet, which is ironic because they were caught out by a risk that they had greater insight into than just about anyone else. Perhaps it is not so surprising when we factor in the large fees generated and the bonuses their staff stood to gain by selling the products. The attraction of short-term gains was too good to pass up and they became either blind to or unwilling to see the risks.

Lehman – holding over US$600 billion in assets – was a monumental failure, and it was the first major bank to file for bankruptcy protection in the sub-prime crisis. It still holds the unenviable record of being the largest bankruptcy in US history. Along with other failures and stresses in the financial sector, the ripples became waves and triggered a recession that impacted the livelihoods of billions of people around the world. While Lehman's volunteering and corporate foundation activities might have been doing good, that good pales into insignificance compared to the damage it wrought through its core business practices. Those impacts can't be ameliorated by a small set of charitable activities and, as a result of this and many other corporate disasters, there's increasing cynicism about business motives. Global communications firm Edelman is well known for surveying the level of trust the general population has in business, not-for-profits, government and the media. More than half of the respondents to a recent survey[17] believed that business CEOs are driven by greed rather than making a positive difference in the world.

Even well-regarded companies can fall from grace due to illegal or immoral corporate practices. Volkswagen was abruptly removed from the Dow Jones Sustainability Index when it was found to be altering emissions data from millions of vehicles. An American executive subsequently received a seven-year jail sentence. It went from a company classified by sustainability experts as being in the top decile worldwide to one that fell out of favour quickly. Unless you're an insider, it's hard to tell exactly what's going on in our biggest corporations and whether they are as good or responsible as they purport to be. Most people working inside them may not know either.

Some companies and industries that have historically been able to keep out of the spotlight are now being subjected to more scrutiny. The partner-owned management consultancy McKinsey & Company was analysed by *New York Times* journalists[18] to find out if it was operating at best practice in line with its stated goals. After a year of investigations they concluded the answer was often no. For example, the Massachusetts Attorney General accused them of instructing the maker of a powerful opioid on how to turbocharge sales and counter the efforts of drug enforcement agencies. This prompted McKinsey's senior partner to send a letter to North American employees outlining how they intend to review their client selection criteria, transparency, accountability, mission, purpose and broader impact. It will be interesting to see if they follow through on their intentions.

Like most large enterprises, McKinsey & Company has a nice looking corporate responsibility page on its website heralding the pro bono work that it does. So how does the public weigh this up against, for example, the role it is playing in the crippling social and health problems that are caused by over prescription of opioids? McKinsey's aspiration to high standards seems to be for public relations purposes rather than a guiding principle for its core business. Being a provider of business-to-business professional services, rather than a highly visible consumer brand, has perhaps allowed this to largely escape attention up until now.

A deficit of trust takes time to restore. The challenge for many corporations is to build or rebuild trust in a genuine and sustainable way. Philanthropy and corporate social responsibility (CSR) agendas, while commendable, cannot repair or build trust when core business practices are the cause of decline. To consider whether there is any genuine impetus for companies behaving badly to change, we'll look at the historical, current and future role of the company.

Farewell shareholder primacy

Companies are at their best when they provide effective solutions for our genuine needs, and at their worst when they grow profits by exploiting people or the planet. They seldom start out with bad intentions; however they can lose their way. My father arrived in Hobart, Tasmania, from England with his parents in 1950 and they set up a corner store in Battery Point – an inner city suburb that is a much more desirable location now than it was back then. His family were its owners, managers and employees, providing a one-stop shop for people's daily grocery needs. For a small business serving a local market, exploiting their customers' trust would have been foolish. Contrast their simple, customer-facing business to that of a global supermarket chain or conglomerate where executives in group headquarters become disconnected from daily interactions with customers. They may be motivated more by career progression and personal gain than genuine care. Who will advocate on the customers' behalf in this scenario? Should the company only focus on maximising profits or seek to satisfy all of the stakeholders it deals with? Or is there another way to balance the profit imperative with customer and community needs? These are challenging and increasingly more relevant questions.

It can be hard getting the right balance between competing interests. We have shareholders wanting profits that may come at the expense of customers, employees, suppliers, the environment or community interests. The first group is putting capital at risk for the prospect of a financial return and the others are exposed to the impacts of the company's operations. Critics of the public company model focus on the asymmetry of risk: shareholders can sell their holding and exit at any time, whereas people living in their shadow cannot divest themselves in an instant[19]. Shareholders have the luxury of being able to further manage their risk by spreading their investments across a wide range of companies, whereas local residents and suppliers don't have that option.

Milton Friedman, the 1976 Nobel Prize-winning economist, took a stance[20] against the idea that companies have social responsibility, arguing that they should focus on maximising profit within the rules of the game because they are not skilled in solving social problems, and that job should be outsourced to government. This is known as shareholder primacy, where the profit agenda is put before everything else. Companies, indeed, may not possess the requisite skills to tackle all of the social problems they come across; however they can form partnerships with social sector organisations to make improvements that also enhance their bottom line. This entity that we call the company comes from society, and its success can only be judged according to its impact on society. The same point was recently made by the Business Roundtable – a group comprising the CEOs of major US companies with US$15 trillion in revenues – who stated[21] that the purpose of the corporation must move away from maximising profits to promoting an economy that serves all. They concluded their statement with:

> *"Each of our stakeholders is essential. We commit to deliver value to all of them, for the future success of our companies, our communities and our country."*

Their stance makes sense because a strong social and economic backdrop is positive for profit growth, and they should have a keen commercial interest in addressing problems that present opportunities for improving profitability or growth. Relying on government or the social sector to fix the problems they face is poor delegation as those entities may not have the level of resources nor motivation to act. If there is a business case for a company to invest in the problems affecting it, then why not take control and do it? Today Friedman's view is considered outdated and flawed by many; however it gives context as to where the current level of corporate distrust and disillusionment with capitalism emanates from.

A more modern approach is evident in Cisco's partnerships with public education institutions to improve the IT capabilities of its future workforce. It is addressing shortages in the skilled workers it needs to support and drive growth by investing in solutions: its Networking Academies[22] have served 7.8 million students and 22,000 educators across 180 countries. A historical example lies in Johnson & Johnson[23] helping employees who wanted to quit smoking, leading to a two-thirds reduction in smokers over a 15-year period. The company profited from higher productivity and estimated savings of US$250 million on healthcare costs alone, with a return of $2.71 for every dollar invested. These examples and more that we'll unpack in this book show that the link between shareholders and stakeholders is not obtuse, and is, in many cases, direct and relevant. I doubt Cisco or Johnson & Johnson would have made progress on their chosen issues by taking a passive approach and leaving it to not-for-profits or government to sort out.

The companies we examine won't all be as pure as the driven snow, because when we look across their vast corporate structures we're likely to find current or historical problems. At the time of writing, Johnson & Johnson finds itself embroiled in lawsuits relating to opioids, blood thinners, pelvic mesh and talcum powder. My contention is that every business should be reducing or removing the externalities that it's responsible for – that's the risk management side of the equation for them – and that they can realise commercial benefits through a genuine commitment to social purpose. For that reason, we must highlight the good, the bad and the ugly aspects of corporate behaviour in our conversations. A virtuous circle can be created between shareholders and society provided companies have the determination and skill to act. We'll be looking more closely at the specific mindset and skills needed to do this in Section III.

Misaligned timeframes

Public company CEOs are in a bind. They may want to build for the future in a sensible and measured way, however they also feel the pressure from market analysts and investors who want to see consistent increases in short-term earnings. These conflicting timeframes can encourage them to pursue shorter-term wins, which in turn may perpetuate activities that are irresponsible, unsustainable or cause harm. This is why the high-profile investor Warren Buffett is amongst those advocating[24] the abolition of quarterly earnings guidance, claiming that it encourages companies to fudge numbers and increases the temptation for financial misbehaviour.

Curiously, some corporate leaders have succeeded despite the shorter-term pressures of running a listed company. Ray Anderson, the founder of Interface, a US carpet and floor tile manufacturer, passed away in 2011. Much has been written[25] about Ray because of his track record as an innovator and paradigm buster. In 1994 he took on the seemingly impossible challenge of creating a zero waste business – which he eventually did. More impressively, Ray had to back his intuition to achieve it. Looking through the numbers to see bigger picture opportunities was the hallmark of his success. The journey that Interface embarked on was not easy. In fact, Ray was quoted as saying that if he had thought about how it might be done before he attempted to do it, there was a fair chance he would have pulled the pin on the whole idea. His gift was an ability to identify and focus on the end result – Mount Sustainability as he called it – and then challenge his co-workers, suppliers and advisors to make it happen. While Ray had an altruistic streak in him, he never doubted that the path he was on would deliver commercial benefits – he could see that eliminating waste would have a big and positive impact on the bottom line.

Under Ray's guidance, Interface proved to be more resilient than its competitors in the 2002-03 downturn, when its sales fell only 17 per cent versus a 30 per cent fall in the industrial carpet market as a whole. How did Ray get all this past a board that might have called his motives into question? He was able to articulate his strategy in the language that investors and the Board could understand, one that connected his sustainability agenda to corporate profitability. At Interface, Ray achieved what many other CEOs have struggled to do: create an ambitious long-term strategy while keeping his board and the market on-side. Most CEOs and boards haven't been so willing or successful. In Section II we'll be creating a more formal language to describe Ray's approach.

Linking corporate profitability to supporting social and environmental challenges is a very effective way of (re)building trust and improving the sustainability of earnings. It doesn't mean other forms of support aren't valued or needed; it's about maximising what companies can bring to the table. We don't need to abandon capitalism, just to use it better. Companies that maintain a profit-at-all-costs mindset have a limited future. Before looking further into the shift in mindset required, let's review the approaches that have been tried thus far.

chapter 2
what's already been tried?

The methods that have been tried range from philanthropy to CSR to new investment styles, reporting approaches and modified organisational structures. The main ones are outlined here, including the reasons why they've had limited impact.

Philanthropy

Most of us are naturally philanthropic and want to give a little or a lot based on our level of wealth, connection to a cause or strength of belief. From a business owner or executive's perspective, giving is regarded as the done thing, and the more successful you are the more people expect you to help out or give back. Corporate philanthropy – usually conducted through a foundation – is about looking after the welfare of others when you're doing well yourself. Most companies' workforce, customers and surrounding community members will have minimum expectations about what they think they should be giving. It's a good way for CEOs and boards to satisfy their consciences – they may be motivated by altruism, enhancing their egos or by the tax deductibility of gifts to registered not-for-profits. Present-day billionaires, including Bill and Melinda Gates and Warren Buffett, have given away tens of billions of dollars, and managing foundation wealth is a business unto itself. These are large contributions, however they are dwarfed by the size and power of the resources that companies can bring through their business-as-usual activities.

Giving is often associated with reducing risk. An international company operating a coal mine not far from where I live is the biggest employer in the area, and it's not surprising that it sponsors the football club and various other local causes. The sponsorship does little to boost its profitability, but being seen to do the right thing helps keep people on-side. The investment reduces the risk of objections to its use of local water resources, general attitudes towards fossil fuels, high asthma rates in the surrounding area (although there's been no conclusive link to the mine's activities) and its trucks rolling through town.

Demonstrating giving power is becoming a high stakes game for companies that compete for the best and brightest talent. Some are contributing one per cent of profits, employee time and equity to causes as a way of attracting employees who want to express their social conscience. These commitments can be very helpful. The counterview is that volunteering days aren't always taken up by employees due to pressure from their managers or a lack of personal prioritisation. A bank branch manager once phoned me to get ideas for a "team activity" they could undertake before the deadline for using their volunteering day lapsed. Up until then we'd had some good discussions about how they could use their time and skills to make a difference in a way that would also benefit their branch performance. As the deadline drew nearer, they just needed a way to get it done as quickly and painlessly as possible, which helped a charity in a fairly predictable, low-impact way.

The benefits of giving and volunteering are not always easy to reconcile as we saw where the Lehman Brothers' case created some good and a lot of bad at the same time. Another example can be seen in the Sackler family, the owners of McKinsey-advised[26] Purdue Pharma in the US. Their company has made huge profits from the sale of OxyContin, the prescription painkiller associated with the opioid crisis. Documents contested by the family have been tendered in court alleging that family members directed company efforts to mislead the public and doctors about the dangers of the drug[27]. With increasing lawsuits, the company has filed for Chapter 11 bankruptcy[28] in an attempt to shield itself from thousands of claims. As a result of the adverse publicity surrounding OxyContin, many art galleries, museums including the Guggenheim in New York, and other charities around the world have refused to take, or returned funds to, the family's foundation.

+ + +

It's fair to question whether corporate and other forms of philanthropy have the capacity to change the world. The evidence is mixed, both in terms of intention and of the quantum of funding needed. As far back as Robert Tressell's dark, satirical 1914 novel *The Ragged-Trousered Philanthropists*, the motives behind industrialists' philanthropic agenda have been questioned. Tressell drew on his own experiences, portraying the wealthy English upper classes as providing enough charity to prevent the workers from falling into the poverty abyss, but not enough to lift them out. More recently, former President of the Rockefeller Foundation Judith Rodin noted that even a continued steady rise in philanthropy would be nowhere near enough to make a difference, observing[29] that the resources, scale and innovation of business are needed in order to make real headway.

Having outlined some limitations of traditional philanthropy, there are more interesting forms such as *catalytic philanthropy* that aim to

25

create transformative change beyond writing the cheque[30]. In other words, the funding is for the purpose of testing new and innovative approaches to problems. Philanthropy is good and there are ways in which it can be utilised to create more impact, but its motives are not always easy to reconcile nor may it always be the most efficient or effective use of funding resources.

Corporate social responsibility and sustainability

At its core, corporate social responsibility is about companies protecting their brand, reputation and social licence to operate. Definitions of CSR vary, and a consensus view[31] is that it's the responsibilities and expectations that society has of organisations: economic, legal, ethical and philanthropic. Companies usually develop programmes, better practices, accreditations and sponsorships to implement their CSR agenda: for example an employee wellbeing programme, improving working conditions, increasing diversity and inclusion, financial literacy programmes for disadvantaged sections of the community, or sponsoring brand-relevant causes or certifications for the responsible sourcing of raw materials, goods or labour.

The term "sustainability" is a larger and more aspirational concept[32], where companies seek to meet the needs of the present without compromising future generations, focusing on the three main pillars of people, planet and profits. Sustainability has a stronger connection to core business and profitability, however it is often used interchangeably with CSR, which makes conversations confusing.

Table 1 sets out a hypothetical set of issues that a bank may be engaged in as part of its CSR or sustainability agenda. It shows the different forms their initiatives can take and how the benefits vary in terms of social impact and scale. It's noticeable how the latter issues in the table are more likely to benefit the bottom line.

Table 1: Analysis of a hypothetical bank's social and environmental initiatives

Area of need	Example of corporate support	Societal benefits	Business benefits
Cancer research	Foundation giving	Funding for research-based cancer breakthroughs	Name association
Sports clubs and associations	Sponsorship	Resourcing for sporting clubs and associations	Name association, brand and reputation
Arts and culture	Sponsorships or donations to non-profit organisations	Resourcing for arts and cultural activities	Name association, brand and reputation
Domestic violence and elder abuse	Help identify risks and follow a referral or reporting process	Reduction in physical, emotional and financial abuse	Brand and reputational benefits
Handling of financial complaints	Fair and transparent processes	Equity in the customer-corporation relationship	Brand and reputational benefits

Area of need	Example of corporate support	Societal benefits	Business benefits
Disadvantaged customer access	Tailoring service delivery for under-served clients	Inclusion in banking and financial services	Brand and reputational benefits
Climate change	Reduce energy consumption in offices and branches	Reduce greenhouse gas emissions	Comply with energy standards and modest return on investment
Climate change	Supporting the development of the green bond market	Linking investors with climate friendly solutions	A foothold in a high growth market opportunity
Employee health and wellbeing	Prevention and better management of physical and mental health	Improved life quality and career longevity	Increased workforce productivity
Financial hardship	Proactively support customers facing hardship	Help alleviate hardship, family break ups, mental health and related issues	A deeper customer relationship and reduced bad debts

To illustrate what an actual corporate sustainability framework looks like, Kimberly-Clark considers[33] five areas: social impact, forests and fibre, waste and recycling, energy and climate, and its supply chain. It has programmes that improve access to sanitation, help children thrive and empower women and girls. Responsible sourcing of forestry underpins forest and fibre programmes along with accreditations and certifications, such as those from the Forest Stewardship Council. These activities serve a purpose: keeping customers, communities and regulators on-side, and maintaining brand value and corporate reputation.

Companies (for the most part!) steer clear of breaching laws, rules and regulations. But there are grey areas where activities are legal but there is harm resulting from them, such as the tobacco and gaming industries. When details are uncovered or activists mount effective campaigns they become significant issues for companies, as Nike found out with respect to the backlash against poor working conditions at many of its Southeast Asian suppliers. The poor publicity led Nike to change its practices and shore up its brand appeal. To give credit where it's due, Nike has been on a path towards best practice, although it is troubling to think that many good corporate initiatives like these emanate from crises and risk reduction goals rather than proactive, value-adding ones.

Whilst CSR sounds good and is a necessary part of every company's agenda, it has limitations. Another illustration comes from the Royal Commission into Misconduct in the Banking, Superannuation and Financial Services Industry in Australia that uncovered widespread dishonesty and illegalities: banks charging fees to the accounts of deceased customers, conflicts of interest in providing financial advice and, in one case, systematic document forgery. Several major banks were found to be maximising shareholder gains to the detriment of their customers' interests. It's not a sustainable model nor does it help in bolstering the low levels of trust in banks. During the inquiry, the extensive CSR programmes of the banks didn't count for much because the damage was occurring in business-as-usual. It goes to the heart of the problem that, for the most part, social considerations are seldom at the core of business strategy. This is compounded by the fact that CSR departments don't generate revenues and therefore their impact is limited by the finite budgets allocated to them. They are viewed as cost centres and seldom invited to the table when strategy is being formed.

Let's next consider some of the approaches that investment managers have used in trying to differentiate good companies from the not-so-good ones.

Ethically screening investments

Whenever companies are caught doing the wrong thing, there's inevitably a chorus demanding that "companies must do good". Even though I agree wholeheartedly with the sentiment, the pragmatist in me knows they aren't going to abandon their profit motive, so what is the alternative? Ethical investing – also known as socially responsible investing – is an approach that tries to influence the ways companies behave. It's where an investment manager or researcher determines which companies are good, according to a defined criteria, and they invest with a natural bias towards the good ones. In many cases they establish lists of 'bad' companies they exclude or take underweight positions in. The idea is that, if more investors become ethical, the supposedly bad companies are penalised because there's less demand for their shares. This increases their funding costs and, as a result, reduces their profitability.

To implement an ethical approach, you first require a definition of what is good and bad, which can be problematic. Next time you're with a group of friends, see if you can reach consensus on where you draw the line. You may agree that companies manufacturing cluster bombs and tobacco products are ones you'd like to avoid; however there may be those that you disagree on. For example, is a company producing alcoholic products bad? How can that be so if we personally enjoy a social drink? Do we distinguish between different types and strengths of liquor? What if they sell alcopop drinks aimed at young drinkers? Is any of this bad or is all of it bad? Is there a threshold level of harm that triggers a rating of bad? What if a company has great, socially progressive products but treats its employees and communities poorly? We don't need to throw out ethical investing as a methodology, just accept that it's hard converting a range of very complex considerations into a yes/no decision.

Another obstacle is transparency – knowing exactly what's going on inside companies. Investors are prone to being blindsided as per the Volkswagen emissions scandal. It's often impossible to know about these risk factors unless you're an insider, and insider trading is illegal. Investors certainly should endeavour to uncover such problems, but must accept that their research depth is limited and they won't ever have perfectly accurate information. As a result, some darlings of the ethical investor market can quickly become pariahs and leave you wondering if your approach really is sound after all.

Materiality is another consideration: when a company is taking a risk or doing something customers or communities don't like, does that warrant a blanket ban or should it depend on how significant the issue is? The pens in your stationary cupboard may not be made from sustainably sourced ink, so should ethical and other investors avoid your company because of that? You may also provide employment for disadvantaged groups and a materiality lens would say the positives far outweigh the negatives, but it won't always be clear-cut using an ethics-based checklist.

While ethics must be a consideration for every company in terms of what's acceptable, relying on a reductionist approach to categorise a company as good or bad doesn't have enough power or consistency on its own to drive large-scale change. Ethical funds have traditionally been a niche product category, although it's easy to see how the skills needed to run them could transfer to other investment approaches.

More investment and reporting based approaches

One of the first challenges to traditional corporate reporting came via the triple bottom line methodology, often abbreviated to TBL or 3BL, the idea being that reporting on social and environmental impacts in addition to financial profit and loss data would promote a better understanding of the societal costs or externalities underpinning profitability. John Elkington coined the phrase in 1994, and in a reflection[34] on its limited success he noted:

> *"Whereas CEOs, CFOs, and other corporate leaders move heaven and earth to ensure that they hit their profit targets, the same is very rarely true of their people and planet targets. Clearly, the Triple Bottom Line has failed to bury the single bottom line paradigm."*

The TBL is conceptually strong: it's the application that is problematic. Apart from some inspired reporting leadership[35] from a handful of companies, executives have historically had little incentive to improve their non-financial reporting. The reality is that when companies review their strategy, times get tough or there's pending merger or acquisition activity, there is little enthusiasm for TBL.

Another approach pursued by investment analysts is to ask companies to report on environmental, social and governance (ESG) risk factors to gauge their level of corporate responsibility. The practice has been championed by the United Nations through its Principles for Responsible Investment, encouraging investors to look deeper into the companies they have shareholdings in. It prompts questions like: how do they source their raw materials or goods? Do the board and management govern with transparency and integrity? Will climate change pose risks for earnings? Are there prevailing societal trends that will impact the business model? It is very useful information, however it has often felt more like a reporting exercise than one shaping investment portfolios or the core strategy of companies.

There are developments in the market that could see ESG analysis become much more influential, as evidenced by BlackRock's Chairman and CEO, Larry Fink, who has signalled[36] a transition to sustainability-themed performance benchmarks. Why is this important? To date, a large portion of BlackRock's funds have been managed against standard stock market indices such as the S&P 500, which include all of the larger listed companies regardless of their longer-term sustainability credentials. Under the new approach, the starting point will be to hold much-reduced weightings in companies like ExxonMobil, due to risks in earnings from fossil fuels, and therefore create significantly less demand for their shares and put greater downward pressure on valuations. With $7 trillion of funds under management, when mainstream firms like BlackRock start making these types of moves it will certainly influence the way company CEOs and boards behave.

Other frameworks you may have heard of include the Global Reporting Initiative: promoting excellence in sustainability reporting through disclosure of corporate impacts in climate change, human rights, governance and social wellbeing. Investment analysts make use of this data in ESG research. And there's the International Integrated Reporting Council, a global collaboration between regulators, companies, investors, not-for-profits, accounting bodies and other standard setters who are attempting to align company invest-ments and behaviours with sustainable development. Their goal is for this data to become part of normal company reporting.

As you can see, there are many methods that focus on identifying social and environmental risks. What's generally missing is a com-mon language and strategy lens that focuses on value creation.

Social enterprise, B-Corps and new financing methods

There are new types of organisational structures and financing methods that help to make a difference. Social enterprises are purpose-driven, not-for-profit entities that derive the majority of their income from commercial sources such as recycling or waste stream management contracts (green waste, recycling mattresses, etc.), retail shop fronts (bargain clothes stores) or disability employment operators providing low-cost labour (manual processing, warehouse packing, printing or posting services). By utilising a not-for-profit model, they aren't under pressure to provide returns to shareholders and because of that, in theory, they can be more competitive because of their lower funding costs. For the same reasons, their access to capital for expansion may be somewhat limited.

Social enterprises tend to be found in markets or industries with low capital intensity, such as manual processing, labour hire or retailing; however a handful of social enterprises manage to break through and become much larger entities. The social enterprise thankyou disrupted the Australian bottled water market, gaining a foothold and applying its profits to global impact partners who deliver safe water and poverty alleviation projects around the world. Their co-founder, Daniel Flynn, describes how they were able to convince a manufacturer to supply their product on generous payment terms so they could get it out to market and use the sales proceeds to meet their production costs. In other words, they got their business up and running with virtually no working capital, and he says it wasn't a ride for the faint-hearted. Several social enterprises have disrupted markets because they have a social purpose that customers are willing to support; they may also benefit from corporate or government procurement policies that allocate a certain amount of spending to them.

Cooperatives and mutuals such as credit unions are enjoying a resurgence, partly due to the higher trust levels they have relative to their for-profit competitors. The well-known Dutch agricultural lender Rabobank is a cooperative with members rather than shareholders, proving that not-for-profit enterprises can reinvest surpluses and become large enterprises. In Australia, the outgoing chief executive of one of our largest member-owned organisations noted[37] that they compete in the same markets and under the same laws and regulations as for-profits, but emphasised the subtle differences when he said "We don't just do things to make money, we make money to do things."

The Yunus Centre makes use of a social business model where investors are allowed to recoup their initial investment, but never receive any dividends. If or when the business generates profits, they are reinvested into the business to further support its social cause. The Grameen Danone Company, a social business based on a partnership between Grameen Bank founded by Muhammad Yunus and the French dairy corporation Danone, produces and sells affordable yogurt products for malnourished children in Bangladesh. This is similar to a social enterprise model.

If you have heard of B-Corps and are wondering what they are, they are best described as a variation on the for-profit model. Directors of companies in the US wishing to build a level of social purpose into their charter felt they were at risk of being prosecuted for breaching their legal duty of maximising shareholder returns. As a result, the creation of B-Corp status permits them to consider the impact of their decisions on their workers, customers, suppliers, community and the environment[38]. Ben & Jerry's ice cream is a well-known example of a B-Corp that maintains this status even now as a subsidiary of Unilever. It sources dairy responsibly and positions its brand around social and environmental activism, which appeals to the spirit of the founders and a rebellious streak in its customers. Outdoor gear brand Patagonia is another B-Corp favourite.

There's a lot of excitement around new financing models such as impact investing and instruments like social impact bonds (SIBs) that are a conduit for funding social outcomes with private capital. If the social programme funded by the bonds works and saves money for government, then a pre-agreed portion of those savings is shared with the private investors, who receive a capped return on their investment. SIBs are issued out of a special entity that is party to a three-way agreement between a group of private investors, a social services contract provider and one or more government departments. For example, if a programme designed to reduce prisoner reoffending rates (recidivism) is successful, savings across government agencies will be widespread because there will be lower demands on the justice system, policing levels, prison facility management costs and so on. Investor returns are at risk if the programme is unsuccessful.

These structures are effective in mobilising private capital for some of our most challenging social problems, although the complexity of the deals and intricacy of their structures mean that transaction costs are high and scale is hard to achieve.

Collective impact projects

Collective impact is the name given to projects that tackle very complex social problems in holistic and considered ways. In Logan, a city in the Australian state of Queensland, the percentage of young children developmentally on track is below the state and national averages, and the Logan Together[39] initiative aims to bridge that gap. A backbone organisation was formed to coordinate a range of support services that span the period from when couples are ready to have kids through to pregnancy, childbirth, and early childhood, up until the kids are eight years old. It involves many organisations and project partners working better together, rather than making their own interventions in an uncoordinated way. It is a powerful methodology and a very skilled process. The practical challenges of collective impact projects include the long timeframes and levels of funding required. Businesses could be involved in these types of projects; however the long timelines might be challenging for them.

+ + +

All of the approaches that have been tried – the methods, models and innovative forms of financing – show there are genuine efforts being made to help solve our pressing needs, although there's been limited success in harnessing the real engine room of businesses to drive change at scale. To do that, we need to create joint ownership of the problems.

chapter 3
a shift in purpose, on purpose

A corporate purpose – usually expressed through a mission, vision or purpose statement – has long been a decorative piece of corporate architecture. There's always a buzz of excitement at the offsite session when the purpose is formed; a phalanx of consultants and advisors will be on hand to manage the process and express confidence that it has been well thought through. And then it tends to disappear from view as everyone goes back to doing business in exactly the same way as before. Not for much longer though. A shift is underway that requires companies to be cleverer and clearer about their purpose if they are to survive and generate sustained profits. How does profit fit in with purpose? Why is that becoming essential? And what does it look like in practice? We'll start with a one word concept that explains the rationale.

Interdependence

Social researcher Hugh Mackay in his book *The Art of Belonging* notes that we as humans don't do so well when we are on our own; we thrive when we form groups or communities that support one another. At the same time, most of us want to elevate our standing within our community. After all, who wants to be on the bottom rung of the social ladder? Because of this, Mackay points to the fundamental tensions between the goals of the individual and the group, and that our success as a species is all about getting that balance right. There is an *interdependent* relationship here, meaning that our individual success is linked to the overall health of the community we live in. Likewise, in his *Theory of Moral Sentiments*, Adam Smith purports that "all the members of human society stand in need of each other's assistance, and are likewise exposed to mutual injuries." The relationship between business and society has the same characteristics: it's about *interdependence* not *independence*.

Because the performance of a business is heavily influenced by the socio-economic conditions surrounding it, the question becomes which challenges should it support and how can it be done? This conversation wasn't so crucial before now, when the natural resources available for economic expansion and growth felt relatively unbounded. Many of the issues we're grappling with today could once be swept under the carpet and out of view. With greater consumer activism and recognition by governments of the cost of externalities, companies can no longer expect to behave independently of society and prosper. They have a choice: to reshape their thinking or not. It's the interdependence of business and society that drove the Business Roundtable to espouse the view that companies must shift from merely keeping stakeholders onside to actually addressing their needs in order to remain relevant and grow. In other words, profit will be the corporate by-product of successfully meeting society's needs. We'll see new types of collaborations and partnerships, and mutual gains will be required to sustain them because they tend to fall away or be ineffective otherwise. Building social capital is central to the task.

Social capital

Humanity is a sea of people who have differing approaches to leading good lives; we differ in the way we want to use the Earth's resources, how we co-exist, and in balancing living-for-now with a positive and sustainable future. The term social capital is used to describe the strength of connections that help our society function effectively. It's the invisible glue that holds us together, and while we may not always appreciate it when it's present, we certainly notice when it's absent. If you've taken time to get to know your neighbours or supported not-for-profits, charities or civic institutions in your area, then you've been helping to build social capital. So, is there a link between social capital and profitable business?

Robert D. Putnam's 1993 paper *Making Democracy Work: Civic Traditions in Modern Italy* puts forward the notion that communities become economically rich *because* they are socially strong, and not the other way around. Putnam studied Northern Italy's history of communities, guilds, clubs and choral societies and found that the social capital they created led to greater community involvement and economic prosperity. Furthermore, the key drivers of social capital were found to be trust, mutual reciprocity and well-defined social norms. Without trust, people go into their shells, disengage, hold back on their best ideas and put in less effort to help others in their community. Mutual reciprocity describes the expectation that a voluntary or discretionary act of help will be repaid at some time in the future, even though no formal contract exists. Social norms are like the unwritten, informal rules that community members expect each other to conform to within reasonable limitations, and they may change over time. The increased attention paid to gender equality, workforce diversity and specific issues like the #MeToo movement has stemmed from changes in community expectations and social norms. Where there are low trust levels, poor expectations of reciprocity and few social norms, people tend to cooperate only when formal rules and regulations are enforced by coercive measures[40]. This creates expensive transaction costs for society. However when social capital is high, crime is relatively low and little policing is needed.

In the corporate world there's growing recognition[41] of the value of social capital, not just in terms of internal communities (workforce), but in guiding the relationships with business partners and stakeholders that will influence their ultimate success or failure. When companies focus on a genuine social purpose, they are helping to build social capital which in turn improves the operating environment and their performance potential. The challenge becomes multidimensional, because they will be dealing with social, environmental and economic outcomes in addition to profitability. To benefit from this, companies need to understand how to work with new partners in sectors they've seldom operated in before. A good example of this can be found in Australia.

A world-changing regional bank

The criteria for company inclusion in *Fortune's* Change the World List are to have annual revenues of US$1 billion or more and be creating positive social impact through core and profitable business. In other words, it's not about social good from philanthropic or corporate social responsibility initiatives; it's about linking societal progress with new and innovative ways of doing business. Let's return to how Bendigo and Adelaide Bank managed to come in at number 13 on the 2017 list.

The banking landscape in Australia includes four large banks that rank first, fourth, fifth and sixth[42] on the stock exchange in terms of size, accounting for nearly a quarter of the value of our top 100 companies. Their size and scale make it hard for smaller banks to compete and capture market share. In the late 1990s – and before Bendigo Bank merged with Adelaide Bank – the four large Australian banks were retreating from rural, regional and suburban areas where their branches were underperforming or unprofitable. As a result, people who lived in these areas would have to drive some distance to access banking services, which also meant they'd be doing more of their shopping and spending away from their home town, and these smaller towns were feeling the pinch of declining trade. Bendigo Bank saw this as an opportunity. However there was no point opening up standard bank branches in places where they weren't viable. Instead they devised an innovative way of directly partnering with local communities to bring a physical branch presence back to town.

How? They launched their community banking model, where a direct partnership is formed with more than 100 local community members who raise capital and become shareholders in an entity that's a joint venture with the bank. The locals take responsibility for marketing, customer acquisition and relationship management, and the bank supplies the systems and infrastructure such as IT, compliance and capital management services. This effectively creates a series of joint ventures with local communities across the country, and in some ways resembles a franchising structure. The bank and local shareholders share revenues and, when these branches become profitable (usually in three to five years), 80 per cent of the local shareholders' dividend is reinvested back into the community by way of grants. At the time of writing[43] [44], that amount had exceeded $200 million. Since the inception of this model, the bank has established more than 300 branches, employed 1,500 staff and drawn upon the expertise and connections of more than 2,000 local directors.

From a commercial perspective, the strategy has generated $34 billion of balance sheet assets, driven higher than average customer growth rates and led to the acquisition of more than one million new customers under the Bendigo Bank brand name, who are benefitting from capital relief (the community contributes the capital) as well as leveraging their existing assets. Their approach is in lock-step with the bank's philosophy[45] of *seeking to feed into prosperity and not off of it*. It has helped them grow to become the fifth largest retail bank in Australia and is a great example of connecting profit growth with social outcomes.

While you may not work in or with the banking sector, such examples are powerful and illustrate how much social impact can be created when companies use purpose as a lens for innovation. You'll see this connection again and again throughout this book. Take, for example, a manufacturer impacted by poor employee health and wellbeing, a lack of affordable housing for workers, insufficient education leading to skill shortages or under-investment in transport infrastructure that prevents people getting to their premises. There could well be a strong business case for them to invest in solutions. Unlocking profits through positive social change won't work when a company is fixated on profit at all costs (or shareholder primacy). A shift in mindset is required to make it work.

Making the shift in purpose, on purpose

Returning to the Edelman Trust Barometer for a moment, another interesting finding is that, despite distrust in big business, 64 per cent of the general public surveyed expect CEOs to lead positive change rather than relying on government to drive it. And more than half of the respondents believe that companies who think only about themselves and their profits are bound to fail. There is a tail-wind for business leaders to experiment and take some risk, which is balanced by the reality that they can often only effect meaningful change when their actions also deliver profits for shareholders. Some companies are commercially savvy enough to innovate and seize the opportunities presented, as we saw with Ray Anderson's company, Interface.

Another example comes from Fuji Xerox, whose ethos of recycling led to the development of closed loop systems and waste management facilities[46]. Fuji Xerox set up an Eco Manufacturing facility in Sydney in the early 2000s, and a subsequent project involving the design of a closed loop packaging system for one of its product lines has helped it achieve an 11-fold return on its original investment of $22 million. Due to its significance, visiting the site is part of its employee induction process. Designing and implementing such systems require a more expansive way of viewing the world and its opportunities. Diagram 1 shows how it's about shifting focus beyond the business systems or value chains that it controls to one that engages with players in the broader ecosystem, like moving from ego-systems to ecosystems. We saw this dynamic at play with the Bendigo and Adelaide Bank, which reached out and formed direct partnerships with local community members to solve a major problem in a profitable way.

Diagram 1: Shifting corporate focus from business systems to ecosystems

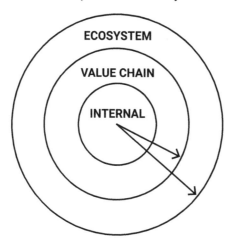

Leading business journals[47] are carrying more commentary about this type of expansive thinking and exploring what new mindsets and management practices are needed. For another illustration of the mindset shift, global publishing company Pearson now refers to itself as *The World's Learning Company*, resulting from an epiphany it had about the way it makes money. Its CEO, John Fallon, explained[48] how it aims to measure product performance according to a social indicator: learning outcomes. Its mission is to make education more accessible and affordable and its purpose[49] is "helping people make progress in their lives through learning." This represents a shift away from chasing incremental growth targets within established product lines, even though Pearson had generally been successful with a growth focus. Fallon could see that maintaining the status quo would be a higher risk approach in the long run, and also knew that such a change would be challenging for Pearson's internal culture. Some hard decisions had to be made about what Pearson kept doing and what it gave up, with subsequent divestments of The Financial Times and the US K-12 textbook-based courseware business along with stakes in The Economist and Penguin Books. The current strategy favours cost-effective digital platforms that engage in the user's learning journey and align better with government education agendas.

Latching onto a great purpose doesn't guarantee results because there are macro trends and competitive forces at play, and any corporate transition plan requires great execution. Pearson's results[50] have been held back by the speed at which it has been able to match consumers' shift to digital products and the lower per unit revenues available in that market. Its focus on learning outcomes, business divestments and shift to digital appear sound; however their experience in implementation hasn't been easy.

To see what a shift in purpose looks like at a grass roots level, in the regional Australian town of Wagga Wagga I've been fortunate to have helped a government department facilitate the shift in thinking that's needed for business, community and government interests to come together to address major challenges. The whole process originated from a conversation between the general manager of a meat processing operation and the local mayor. The company runs an integrated beef processing facility – livestock manager, butcher and meat processor – and it struggles to find enough willing and able entry-level workers for its expanding workforce. The problem is hampering its financial performance in terms of production scheduling, customer satisfaction, productivity, employment costs and retention rates. At the same time, youth unemployment rates are high in the town's social housing estate areas. The community as a whole wants to see more people employed, so there is a potential win-win here. The aim of our project is to link unemployed people who may be suited to this type of entry-level work with greater awareness and easier access to the opportunity – thus increasing the company's workforce depth and solving a commercial problem, decreasing unemployment rates and, ultimately, boosting the social and economic independence of local youth.

There are many reasons why some young people aren't able to find employment, such as illiteracy, lack of familiarity with work culture (some have grown up in families where five successive generations have never held down a job), criminal records, health problems, disability, pressure from family and friends, mental health challenges or drug and alcohol dependencies. It's important to emphasise that this isn't about creating an expensive government-funded employment programme; it's about helping the existing players – such as the company, community centres, social support services, job services providers, schools, police, justice department, health facilities and many more – work together better and create their own self-sustaining solutions. Because there is the prospect of financial upside for the company, we were confident it would be willing to make a decent investment in time and resources. The community will support the project if it trusts the people and the organisations involved. I'll provide more snippets from this project later on, but its scope has expanded beyond this particular meat processing business to include all employers in the town seeking entry-level workers.

All the examples presented here are from companies relishing the opportunity to work with new partners in new ways to ultimately improve performance and gain commercial advantages. Viewing social and environmental challenges as new sources of profitability or growth is the key to mainstreaming the shift from profit-at-all-costs to profit with purpose. Our society will be at its best when companies are competing to provide the most effective solutions to our problems.

The shift is simple and straightforward: embrace the interdependence between companies and society, acknowledge that their fortunes are closely linked, and act in a way that dissolves the tension between profit and purpose, making it an additive process rather than a win-lose game. Doing that requires an ability to innovate, collaborate and address social or environmental issues using a business case. While the concept of combining profit with purpose itself is not new, the language or framework we'll be using has only recently been for-malised in management circles.

The next step is to give it a name.

SECTION II
creating shared value

As we've seen, the methodologies that companies have traditionally used for doing good in society are admirable but not effective. In the main it's because they aren't linked to profitability in a meaningful way, however we've also seen some examples that illustrate the power of connecting profit with purpose. So let's now look at how we formalise our thinking around these more exciting and value adding business opportunities.

chapter 4

the new frontier
for competition

An example from a well-known chocolate brand proves that the concept we are talking about has been around for a long time and provides insight into the principles that interest us.

The Cadbury story

George Frappell arrived by boat in Hobart, the capital of Australia's smallest state, Tasmania, in 1921. He had emigrated from England with his young family aboard the cargo ship Port Darwin to take up what many of us would consider a dream job at the newly built Cadbury chocolate factory: Production Manager, Soft Centres. George was my great-grandfather, and one of many relatives who spent much of their lives working there.

The company had been founded by John Cadbury, who began selling tea, coffee and drinking chocolate on the streets of Birmingham in 1824. It was only a small business and, by the time his two sons, Richard and George, took over in 1861, it was struggling financially.

The number of employees had fallen from 20 at its peak down to 11. The two sons were smart operators and they narrowed the company's focus to cocoa-based products, tested new cocoa bean varieties and invested in modern machinery and processing technologies.

The business turned around, so much so that by 1878 it had outgrown its inner city premises and moved to a new location on the outskirts with more space and closer to transport routes. Over the ensuing years George Cadbury purchased an additional 330 acres of land, upon which he built a model village of more than 300 cottages by the turn of the century. The cottages were let out at affordable rents to employees and their families. If you've ever seen Cadbury cocoa products in your local supermarket aisle, you may be familiar with the name of the estate from the cocoa brand *Bournville*. Millions of people travelled from far and wide to see and experience the model village.

Why did he do it? George believed the provision of good quality, affordable housing, excellent facilities and great services meant workers would not only be happier and healthier, they'd be a more productive and innovative workforce. Addressing genuine societal needs was built into the Cadburys' upbringing and education. Instead of donations to charities unrelated to their operations, they saw an opportunity to combine their social and business goals. Investing in affordable housing for workers was not just a nice thing to do, it was also motivated by business performance, competitiveness and return on investment.

History provides similar examples in retail brands. Milton Hershey was so impressed with the Cadbury estate that he built[51] a village on a grander scale, more akin to a theme park, in Pennsylvania. He didn't need to spend money on advertising for 60 years because of his word-of-mouth reputation for treating employees well. Likewise Tomas Bata, the Czech founder of the Bata Shoe Company, believed in investing in the wellbeing of employees to lower production costs, and built up a vibrant and profitable company. He was known as the Henry Ford of Eastern Europe.

These examples reflect a form of corporate innovation called "creating shared value", often abbreviated to "shared value". The term was defined by Harvard Business School's Professor Michael Porter and strategic philanthropist Mark Kramer, and has helped generate a movement that is flourishing in many parts of the world. Helen Steel, the CEO of Australia's peak practice body *The Shared Value Project,* explains "If doing business with a clear social purpose is the why, then shared value is the how"[52].

Diagram 2: The intersection of business and societal goals

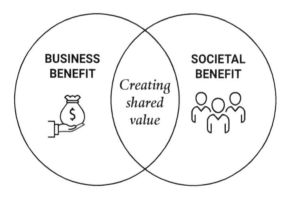

The simplest way of visualising the principles employed at Cadbury is shown in Diagram 2, where the two circles intersect at the point of overlap between the commercial and societal agendas. Shared value principles underpin many of the examples we've unpacked along the way: Bendigo and Adelaide Bank's community bank model, Cisco's education partnerships, Johnson & Johnson's quit smoking campaign, Interface carpets' zero waste goal, Pearson's learning outcomes, Fuji Xerox's Eco-Manufacturing facility and the employment project I've been assisting in Wagga Wagga. They are all about creating shared value.

Why is 'value' the focus of our discussion?

When we walk into a store to buy a pair of shoes, we are faced with a value-based decision. Is the pair of shoes we like going to be good value for the price tag on it? If the same shoes are on sale for a lower price in another shop then they are better value. Having the pair of shoes is a benefit, however benefit alone does not convey value; we can only make judgements about value when we know the price or the cost incurred in obtaining the shoes.

When companies create a business case, they are evaluating the expected benefits relative to the cost of creating them. Even their social initiatives can be viewed through the same value lens: they may deliver a high ratio of benefits compared to cost (good value), or at other times the ratio may be quite low (poor value). Take the example of a work team travelling to a foreign country to do a bike ride and raise $10,000 for an orphanage. The headline amount may sound good, but it's not so good if it costs $20,000 for the team to get there and back. Or suppose a company donates to a charity that helps get young people living on the street into accommodation and they assist 10 youths throughout the year. That may not sound so great if their total budget was $10 million. It is wise to focus on value for evaluation purposes.

What is shared value?

Personally, I like to use the following definition of shared value because it strikes a chord with a wide audience:

"Contributing to positive societal outcomes through core and profitable business."

Mixing profit and purpose can, at face value, be tricky. It raises new questions of whether it is acceptable to make a profit from addressing societal challenges. The question on the flip side is: what incentive is there for a company to help address a societal problem for a sustained period of time if there is no link to profitability? If George Cadbury hadn't seen a link between housing affordability and workforce pro-ductivity, would he have been willing to invest on such a grand scale? If the Bendigo and Adelaide Bank's community bank model had had no commercial incentive, it might only have provided token support to communities in need. When societal issues become strategic con-cerns, companies' interest and care factors increase. Shared value principles are not without their detractors though, so I've provided useful responses to frequent criticisms in the Appendix.

Some businesses historically viewed as 'bad' have also made major contributions to social progress. For example, Nestlé lives in the memories of baby boomers for hooking mothers in developing countries on infant milk formula in the 1970s. On the other hand, it has made major investments in smallholder farmers and Indian milk districts dating back to the 1920s. By the first decade of this century, observers sensed that the company had lost its way[53] and activists were increasingly challenging aspects of its business. Chairman Peter Brabeck-Letmathe lamented that he felt like they were just patching up things through their CSR agenda rather than creating real value for customers and society. Inspired by a conference hosted by Michael Porter and Mark Kramer's consulting firm FSG, Nestlé identified the shared value concept as a core corporate goal. This led to the selection of three priority issues on which to focus: rural development, water use and nutrition. While there will be ongoing debates about Nestlé's past and current actions, that's a healthy guiding light for a company to adopt in charting its future path. Reorganising around purpose should, in theory, produce more sustained results compared to organising around financial targets.

My journey to shared value

During my own corporate career, I became disillusioned with CSR as a way of making positive change at scale. It seemed nice that companies act, but soon became clear that it wouldn't be enough to combat the magnitude of the local and global challenges we are facing. The annual CSR spend of Fortune's Global 500 companies is estimated[54] at US$20 billion, which represents[55] less than one-tenth of one per cent of their revenues and not quite one per cent of their profits. If shared value is embraced as a core management and strategic discipline, there will be dramatic scope to increase this amount.

I stumbled across the shared value concept two years after quitting my job in the investment industry and setting up my own consulting business. During a client assignment, I discovered a *Harvard Business Review* paper called *Strategy & Society*, co-authored by Porter & Kramer that described the concept in a more formal way. I knew that I had found the missing link between profit and purpose.

They coined the term "shared value" in this early paper to describe the intersection of corporate and community agendas, as per Diagram 2. There were three examples that stuck in my mind: Toyota inventing the Prius, a popular car model that reduced greenhouse gas emissions; its hybrid engine was far more efficient and emissions friendly than traditional engines. The Prius became profitable[56] and positioned Toyota as the clear leader in the market for hybrid and electric vehicles. Such was the size of this advance that Toyota licensed its technology to other carmakers. It created a commercial benefit from taking on a global environmental challenge.

The second example was Marriott International, the hotel group, applying shared value principles to the challenge of excessive entry-level employee turnover. It partnered with local community organisations to recruit suitable long-term unemployed candidates for a 180-hour training programme. Ninety percent of trainees in the programme took jobs with Marriott and a year later two-thirds still worked for the group, representing a substantially higher retention rate compared to the standard recruitment model. In net terms, Marriott saved money, increased retention and improved service levels. Addressing a societal challenge produced a return on investment for them too.

Thirdly, Microsoft established a partnership with the association representing community colleges across the US to improve and standardise IT curricula, provide funding for equipment upgrades and send staff volunteers to colleges to help out. Similar to the Cisco example, Microsoft's US$50 million five-year programme was addressing a major industry problem: the shortage of skilled IT workers that was constraining their industry growth prospects. What might look like a CSR programme at first glance had a strong link to its strategic agenda of investing in workforce development to support growth in the industry. This also has the characteristics of a shared value initiative.

Their paper electrified me! The authors showed how the right mindset and innovation skills can unlock profit through purpose. I got so excited that I went on reading about it, and started working on ways of applying the principles to my own clients.

The seminal paper on creating shared value

Building my own business focusing on shared value was tough though, because change usually starts at the top and I didn't have the access to CEOs and boardrooms that Michael Porter, Mark Kramer and FSG enjoyed. I took on consulting work with companies and organisations where shared value principles were useful, while simultaneously suffering the pinch of a dwindling bank balance! At home our dinner menu had transitioned from organic lamb cutlets to wholesome bean and vegetable stew. In the meantime, Porter & Kramer were penning their seminal paper, *Creating Shared Value*, that would appear in the *Harvard Business Review* in 2011, adding to their earlier work and formalising the concept.

A year later I was still blogging on this topic and my income was as variable as the breeze. As it turned out, the universe was looking out for me, because in August a piece I wrote for an online publication entitled *The Missing Link to a Sustainable Future* was retweeted by Michael Porter to his 40,000 plus followers. Not bad when the size of my follower list was less than one per cent of that. Its key message was about shared value being equivalent to the carrot dangling in front of companies to induce greater investment in societal challenges, rather than the stick, which is where they feel compelled to do good by virtue of a threat of brand damage or adverse regulation.

Later that year the authors, via their consulting firm, reached out to a range of global enthusiasts and invited us to join them and their team in Boston to help form a practitioner network. Given my passion for the subject, I was looking forward to learning more about tools and techniques they'd devised in helping companies apply the principles. I found myself borrowing techniques from this and other disciplines and, ultimately, created my own methods for helping clients with their challenges. They form the basis for the processes outlined in Section III.

Not many companies were seeking consulting services at that time, because they didn't really know what shared value strategies were and had little reason to prioritise them as something they needed to do. Even when they did express interest, there was often confusion over what they really were and how they could benefit, which is partly why we'll revisit the differences between shared value and CSR in more detail in Chapter 6. It's hard to put the principles into practice when there are inconsistent levels of understanding.

Nevertheless, interest was growing albeit from a low base. I found the principles could be applied in many different situations to great effect. For example, in analysing and writing up summaries for packaging industry award winners[57], we highlighted the business benefits of the award-winning projects – making the point that there are commercial advantages to sustainability. Prior to that, the industry narrative had been around the environmental benefits alone. It was a subtle yet important shift in the way they talked about their achievements, and an approach that helped increase the level of CEO engagement in sustainability projects. When describing Fuji Xerox Australia's closed loop system, we emphasised its 11-fold return on investment from the Eco Manufacturing Centre. Another packaging award winner, the biopharma group Bristol-Myers Squibb, collaborated with a logistics partner to devise reusable cool packs for temperature-sensitive medicines, eliminating the consumption of disposable coolers, reducing 87 tonnes of landfill and realising tangible savings for its business.

Other examples of assignments I took on where shared value principles were useful included a crisis charity that needed to ramp up its strategic corporate partnerships after losing the backing of a major philanthropic supporter, a credit union that needed to develop a point of difference, a non-profit organisation that needed to broker more effective partnerships between schools and employers, and an aged care operator that sought to diversify income streams and reduce costs due to a forecast downturn in bequests. Shared value principles were very helpful in broadening peoples' ideas about what was possible, and they led us into previously unexplored spaces.

Teething problems

When a new trend comes along, most of us try and catch on as quickly as we can. In the two years following the release of Porter & Kramer's seminal paper, its principles started gaining more attention in corporate and not-for-profit spheres. Many senior executives and managers decided that their CSR initiatives had, all of a sudden, become great illustrations of shared value. In some cases it was true; in most it was not. For the latter group it was about wanting to be seen to be attached to the new trend rather than changing their approach.

In partnership with Allan Ryan's Hargraves Institute (focusing on enterprise innovation), we convened a study group consisting of CSR managers from six major companies and corporate relationship managers from two charities to explore how the principles were currently being used (if at all) and how they could be better applied. We had some moment-of-truth conversations, because most of the companies were good at demonstrating the social and environmental aspects of their programmes and not so good at proving the business benefit. When asked what the business benefit was, the default answer would invariably be "People will see that we are doing good things in the community and they'll buy more of our products", which invited the question "How do you actually measure and attribute those benefits?" This was usually met with silence. Our conversations were highlighting how important it is to gain the right foundation skills, create a business case and put measurement systems in place when applying a shared value lens; otherwise you don't know if it's working or not.

Formal definitions of shared value

Porter & Kramer point to the mutual dependence, or interdependence, of business and society as justifying the need for shared value principles[58]. This is predicated on the fact that societal needs – not just economic needs – define markets, and that they may impose costs on companies or present new product and market opportunities. They provide the following definition "...the principle of shared value, which involves creating economic value in a way that also creates value for society by addressing its needs and challenges", and then extra guidance with "...policies and operating practices that enhance the competitiveness of a company while simultaneously advancing the economic and social conditions in the communities in which it operates."

As mentioned earlier, I prefer to use a simpler and more straightforward description, namely that companies create shared value by "contributing to positive societal outcomes through core and profitable business", because it's important this new language is accessible to a wide audience.

Implicit in these definitions are the two key criteria for the existence of shared value (or not): that there must be both a commercial benefit and a societal gain. The criteria is quite broad and there is no standard methodology for reporting on shared value creation. Each company, its key business partners and stakeholders can agree between themselves on what needs to be measured and reported on. Keep in mind that the purpose of measurement is to inform management about the effectiveness of their investments, and not to drive public relations campaigns.

When applying the principles, we can think of the business benefits as being like any other form of benefits such as revenues from new products, the creation of new markets, increased market share or market growth. They may come in the form of brand value enhancement (providing there is a clear and measurable link) or in the form of cost reductions in sourcing, production or distribution processes; they may be about improving employee productivity or retention rates, or accessing new sources of finance or capital. We saw how Bendigo's Community Bank strategy included customer acquisition, higher than system average growth rates, and balance sheet growth as well as a new source of off-balance sheet capital (i.e. from the community shareholders). The Toyota Prius and its licensed technology provided revenue growth and market leadership, and Microsoft's support for community colleges was underpinned by improving the skills of the employment pool to support its future growth. Marriott's upfront investment in training long-term unemployed cohorts was aimed at decreasing employment and turnover costs.

Positive contributions to society can also come in many forms such as employment, housing, health, education, minimising waste or reducing greenhouse gas emissions. The Sustainable Development Goals (SDGs) provide a good framework for categorising societal needs and benefits. For example, goal 8 deals with jobs and economic growth, which is a theme in the Microsoft, Marriott and Bendigo Community Bank examples. In general, your measurement system needs to be good enough to show that the desired outcomes are being created and I would argue that they should not be so prescriptive, complex or onerous as to deter companies from taking action. Positive action without perfect measurement and evaluation should be acceptable. There's more discussion of measurement in Section III.

Getting an edge

George Cadbury's mindset in the late 1800s confirms the idea of win-win for business and society is not new, nor do the creators of the shared value term claim it is the case. So, why is it timely? And why have there been detractors?

Because of the breakdown in trust between the public and corporations, more sophisticated methods are required to (re)build it. Professor Michael Porter's influence has increased the level of buy-in from executives and directors, and the principles now feature in the syllabus of many post-graduate courses – at the Harvard Business School and University of NSW Business School amongst others. The work of Porter & Kramer has also separated the more strategic, value-adding types of initiatives that were previously bundled in with CSR from the brand and reputation enhancing ones.

With management experts and surveys pointing to the need for CEOs to develop more collaborative and inclusive business models, shared value is a practical framework for bringing them to life. Given the scale of the global challenges we face coupled with business legitimacy concerns, I firmly believe shared value will be the new frontier for competition. The strategies we've already looked at require new mindsets, skills and partnerships, so the companies that get really good at shared value stand to create significant competitive and performance advantages. Gary Cohen of Becton Dickinson – another company we'll examine later on – noted[59] that it is much harder to copy a business model and the relationships that go with it than it is to copy a product.

To illustrate the potential, Bendigo's Community Bank model hasn't faced any serious competitive response because it isn't attractive to the big banks (not enough scale), and their first mover advantage has discouraged smaller banks. This advantage won't last forever because the increasing penetration of online banking means they will eventually need to reconfigure and drive higher returns from their retail spaces. As with any innovation cycle, the value a company creates through a particular initiative will likely decline over time as the market backdrop changes or competitive responses emerge.

There are several mindset features – or preconditions – required for creating shared value. It's worth noting we've covered the key ones already: appreciating the interdependence, not independence, of business and society, and the shift in focus from business systems to ecosystems. We should always keep in mind shared value is merely one lens – albeit a very effective one – that helps in identifying and developing new forms of profitable business, and we'll now look at more examples of the principles in action.

chapter 5
a new lens for innovation

Innovation is a necessity, but drawing inspiration from social and environmental challenges is new for many companies. The end result could be a startlingly successful new line of business through to reduced supply chain costs or greater attraction and retention of top talent. It can be accomplished by a company going it alone in a bid to get advantages over its peers, working with peers on a shared problem or collaborating more broadly at an industry, economic or regional level. The strategy may manifest anywhere in the value chain, which is why shared value is both an exciting and bewildering concept at the same time. The skill lies in finding the parts of your business where societal issues are imposing the greatest costs or presenting the best opportunities and then developing your ideas in an efficient and effective way.

Documenting shared value case studies can also be tricky, partly because commercial sensitivities may deter companies from willingly sharing details, and partly because when they were developed there may not have been measurement or reporting systems in place.

The examples that follow are intended to convey the essence of the win-win approach and how the intention goes beyond traditional CSR programmes and philanthropy. Some of them may look like fairly standard corporate innovations... because they are. The features underlying each example are transportable to other contexts and situations, so I suggest you focus on how they can inform your own approach and opportunities.

Nestlé and Uncle Toby's Oats

An iconic brand among Australians who enjoy oatmeal-based meals such as porridge is Nestlé's Uncle Toby's Oats, one of the largest buyers of oats in the Oceania region with annual procurement requirements of approximately 30,000 metric tonnes. However local farmers had cut back plantings over the past 20 years because of inconsistent yields and uncertain prices. The Uncle Toby's brand was therefore exposed to the variable quality and price volatility that comes with importation as well as transportation costs. The company estimated that all these factors increased input costs by 30 per cent over local sourcing.

Recognising a reduction in costs as a potential opportunity, it began developing closer relationships with growers and grain traders, cultivating a partnership with a key research body, the South Australia Research and Development Institute (SARDI). Having analysed the problem in more detail, Uncle Toby's management found that the uncertainty of disease and drought meant farmers' returns from growing oats were typically lower than those from other crops. Through its partnership with SARDI, it assisted in the development of higher yielding disease and drought resistant varieties. And because farm-specific attributes also affect crop yields, the company built relationships with local agronomists to help farmers in their planning processes.

To reduce financial risk for farmers, a new contract was developed that provided relief in the event that drought or heavy rain affects their ability to harvest and deliver. Uncle Toby's is now sourcing half of its supply from within 100 kilometres of its factory in Wahgunyah, Victoria, and farmers have an attractive alternative crop that comes with technical support and contract flexibility. This outcome[60] is a result of Nestlé's proactive approach to developing its supply chain by supporting growers in close proximity to the factory to strengthen local production as well as diversifying their crop base. A key challenge in this strategy was the long timeframe between investment in research and development and the release of new oat varieties – up to 15 to 20 years. Another challenge was keeping management further up the line engaged in a project that took a long time to evolve. Anecdotally, people living in the region say that the economic uplift has also helped reduce the incidence of mental health problems and suicide. We often criticise corporations for their short-term timelines and should acknowledge this is not always the case.

Embedding shared value principles across IAG

There is a strong incentive to embrace shared value in the insurance sector, because small reductions in the frequency or severity of insurance claims can result in large increases in profitability. IAG is a multinational general insurance company headquartered in Australia that counts Warren Buffett's Berkshire Hathaway as a business partner and shareholder, and ranks as a top 20 stock in the local market. IAG has applied shared value principles across the entire business[61] in a bid to create a platform for sustainable growth. It describes its reason for existence in social terms: "we make your world a safer place", meaning that everything it does for customers must align with this overarching goal. You'll notice its purpose does not limit it to traditional insurance products, providing scope to innovate and explore adjacent markets and opportunities. It has also appeared in a *Fortune Change the World List* for proactive work in addressing driver safety by testing new car models, theft reduction initiatives and collaborating with local government to improve road accident black spots. It shares data with car manufacturers to encourage and assist car safety improvements, offering insurance premium discounts for customers driving certain models.

IAG is one of the few insurers in the region to have an in-house natural perils team, which focuses on climate data and customer impacts. It was a founding member of a multi-sector collaboration known as the Australian Business Roundtable[62] (ABR) for Disaster Resilience & Safer Communities, formed after an unprecedented number of floods, storms and bushfires in Australia. IAG supports the development of a more sustainable, coordinated national approach to disasters caused by natural hazards, working with government and other organisations to effect changes in public policy that increase resilience to adverse weather events. The total economic cost of natural disasters in Australia averages $18.2 billion each year and is projected to rise to $39 billion by 2050[63]. Carefully targeted investments of $250 million per year in preventative infrastructure should reduce these costs by 50 per cent, generating savings of $12.2 billion by 2050. In 2015, the ABR was the first private sector organisation to be awarded the Certificate of Distinction in the 30-year history of the United Nations Sasakawa Award for Disaster Risk Reduction.

IAG has also led the Global Resilience Project as part of its commitment to the UN Principles for Sustainable Insurance initiative. A global risk map identifies the most vulnerable regions and countries based on major natural disasters over the past 115 years. The next phase will focus on effective investments in pre-disaster resilience. A by-product of this work is the creation of more affordable, accessible and scalable insurance solutions.

Apart from the physical aspects of disaster prevention such as encouraging roof gutter cleaning, bushfire risk reduction and supporting emergency services to minimise the impact on residents, IAG knows from experience that socially strong communities respond much more quickly and effectively after natural disasters. They are more likely to be self-organising and take ownership of parts of the process, which significantly reduces claims and recovery costs. IAG decided to investigate if and how it could help build the social fabric of communities in advance of such events. This may sound ambitious, however, with the incentive of a decent return on investment, it's a pathway IAG wanted to explore. One of its pilot projects (Good 'Hood incubators) is in Blacktown in Western Sydney, where in engaging with community interests over an extended period to gain trust, it has found some opportunities, for example, by partnering with Catalysr who help highly skilled and motivated refugees and migrants develop their own businesses. Empowering 'migrapreneurs' to bring their business ideas to life and participate in economic opportunities aligns well with IAG's business insurance brands.

Lion and mid-strength beer

At a recent conference, a panel of managing directors of global food and beverage brands[64] put out a consistent message: their business model needs to change from a boilerplate approach of creating and scaling up brands to one that is more consumer-centric, and be there with the right products at the right time in response to changing needs. They said very frankly they know what the end goal looks like, but they have little idea of how they will get there.

One firm leading efforts in that sector is Lion, a wholly owned subsidiary of the Japanese company Kirin. They've even worked out how to make shared value relevant to beer. Misuse and abuse of alcohol is a serious social problem in Australia with links to assault, domestic violence, drink driving and poor personal health. As a food and beverage brand with alcoholic drinks in its stable, Lion saw an opportunity in the trend towards lower alcohol products. They created XXXX (pronounced 'four-ex') Gold, a mid-strength beer that quickly became the largest selling brand in a very crowded and competitive beer market. It's promoted like a full-strength beer to overcome consumer perceptions of a compromise in taste, and it's a profitable way of playing a role in addressing a social problem.

This innovation is the sort of thing that companies like Lion scout for on a daily basis. With a shared value mindset comes a systematic approach to looking for opportunities rather than relying on chance. It's both an offensive and defensive play, encouraging Lion to follow social trends and anticipate emerging opportunities as well as reducing risks of product and brand obsolescence.

Herbert Smith Freehills (HSF), and its diversity and inclusion agenda

Professional services firms, in general, run on an engine room of talented employees and partners. They do not manage capital intensive operations or projects themselves, although they provide services for clients who do. They can play an important role in creating shared value by assisting their clients and in tackling challenges within their own workforce.

In a discussion with Sue Gilchrist, global council member and head of intellectual property in Australia at international law firm HSF, she outlined its intuitive application of shared value principles. Diversity and inclusion are high on the HSF agenda with a senior partner heading up their global team. At an industry level, HSF participates in a managing partners' forum in Australia that provides a useful platform for discussions and raising standards across the industry.

HSF has made a concerted effort to develop skills and capabilities and take leadership in this area. As a result, it is often sought out by other law firms and clients for advice.

Its agenda is driven from the top down with global CEO Mark Rigotti explaining[65] how, in researching their top 20 customers, HSF gained insights into the value of diverse teams. One construction sector client explained how HSF's representatives "didn't look like them" when they came in and pitched for business, which was a powerful message to take on board. By increasing diversity, HSF brings a wider range of talents and skills to clients – many of whom have diversity and inclusion agendas themselves.

HSF believes that taking genuine interest in diversity and inclusion and culturally embedding this in the workplace drives higher retention rates and commercial advantage. HSF likes to ask why people stay more than pondering why they leave. Key challenges include helping female lawyers break through the promotion ceiling, preventing and supporting mental health problems and addressing imbalances in the cultural make-up of the workforce. With more Asian law students and Asian-based clientele, HSF is conscious that it has relatively few partners with Asian backgrounds and it's smart to bridge this gap. These are all areas where HSF links commercial opportunity to changing social attitudes and preferences.

What is the key ingredient for professional services firms to embrace this type of thinking? Sue believes it is strong leadership from the board and CEO, and collaborating closely with clients and colleagues on these issues.

CJ Korea Express Senior Parcel Delivery

Korea is on track to have the second oldest population in the world by 2050, with the proportion of senior citizens set to rise from the current level of 12 per cent to 37 per cent. The consequences of an ageing populating include social isolation, poverty, health and well-being issues and intergenerational disconnection. CJ Korea Express is growing rapidly as a global integrated logistics company and has four business areas: contract logistics, parcel delivery, maritime business and forwarding services. The express parcel service faced a shortage of staff and challenges in completing the last mile of the delivery process in remote areas and where there are narrow lanes and alleyways in towns. Standard vehicles could not access delivery addresses and the company had to use high-priced call-van services to fill the gap. The connection of the business problem to the social opportunity led to the Senior Parcel Delivery service being established[66].

Previous attempts to overcome the challenge were driven from the CSR agenda, however the system lacked the integrity and efficiency required to produce results. A new partnership between CJ Korea Express, the Korean Ministry of Health & Welfare and several municipal governments saw the creation of a seniors-based stand-alone service with delivery centres situated near apartment complexes and residential areas. Electric carts enable deliveries in tight-access areas and have increased average parcel volumes by nearly 70 per cent. From a business perspective, CJ Korea Express has increased its processing and delivery capacity and created 560 new jobs for seniors within three years of inception. It plans to expand the initiative nationwide.

This example highlights the key feature of the innovation process: finding a profitable solution to both a social and corporate challenge. After failed attempts to address the problem through the CSR agenda, a partnership-based model has worked. The United Nations has recognised the Senior Parcel Delivery service as a leading case of using shared value principles to address its Sustainable Development Goals.

Boosting profitability by re-purposing food waste at Blantyre Farms

Blantyre Farms is a mixed farming and livestock business situated near the town of Young in New South Wales, incorporating broad-acre cropping of wheat, barley and canola, with beef, wool and lamb production, and a large and intensive indoor piggery[67]. It employs 40 staff, produces 40,000 pigs each year and has an annual turnover of approximately $14 million. Almost all of its 2,000-3,000 tonnes of annual grain production are utilised for pig feed. Edwina Beveridge and her husband Michael took over the business from her parents in 2007 and have advanced it substantially.

With a downturn in pork prices of 40 per cent in 2017 caused by oversupply and improved production methods, many pig farmers have struggled to remain viable, and managing input costs is critical to their survival and competitiveness. Several years ago they found that they could ramp up their use of food waste as pig feed. By successfully building relationships with food companies, they meet the 7,500 (dry) tonne shortfall largely through food that is past its shelf life or use-by date but still suitable as pig feed. The only real alternative for this waste stream has been landfill at a cost of $300 per tonne or more to the manufacturer versus a much lower (on average) estimated cost of $75 per tonne in redirecting it to Blantyre Farms. The nutritional value of the food waste determines whether the manufacturer is required to pay freight and handling costs or whether Blantyre must absorb these. Edwina calculates the average saving at $880,000 per annum – which significantly improves profitability.

In 2011, the farm started generating its own renewable electricity by capturing the methane gas from manure, meeting 100 per cent of their needs and saving the business about $29,000 a month. In fact, excess amounts are sold into the grid to generate extra revenue and energy-related initiatives are adding nearly $600,000 per annum to the bottom line. These sustainability initiatives have seen relationships with major clients evolve into value-adding partnerships. For example, a major supermarket buyer regards Blantyre Farms as progressive and innovative, and its model is one that its consumers are really interested in.

Overall, food waste is being diverted from landfill each year and used to support pork production, with by-products used for electricity generation. Edwina notes that their environmental footprint is now 95 per cent lower than the average pork producer and, coupled with the considerable increase in profitability, it meets the criteria of creating shared value.

Enel Green Power

The energy industry is one where emerging products and solutions tend to be well aligned with environmental challenges. Investing in renewable energy is a pathway to reducing emissions – what's not so easy is creating a commercial business around it. Enel Power was founded as an electric utility company in Rome in the 1960s with subsidiary Enel Green Power created in 2008. The company recognises that energy is an enabler of social and economic development with 1.3 billion people worldwide lacking access, and getting energy to them has traditionally required new plant and more greenhouse gas emissions. The company set out to provide access to affordable, reliable and clean energy,[68] and now has a presence in 30 countries with nearly as much installed capacity as the entire Australian energy market.

Evaluating new opportunities is core to Enel's process and it looks for locations all over the world where the main stakeholders are keen on renewables and there's a viable business model. It recently identified more than 500 opportunities to establish new renewable generation sources or upgrade existing assets. A 275 megawatt Bungala solar farm development near Port Augusta in South Australia illustrates the application of shared value principles[69] on two levels. Firstly, with increasing demand for renewable energy from wholesale and retail customers, Enel is helping to fill energy supply gaps. Secondly, it engages with the local indigenous community to develop a sustainable workforce during construction and into the operational phase. Antonio Cammisecra, Head of Enel Green Power, notes that producing renewable energy is not the same as being a sustainable operation, and Enel looks at what it can do across the entire business from development to construction and operations to achieve its goals. At the Bungala solar farm this includes investment in indigenous workforce training and development.

From a global perspective, Enel has learned that it is good at developing solutions in a variety of locations and operating environments. Internally, it was difficult for them to break down the perception that sustainable energy is only funded by philanthropy, sponsorships or other compensation arrangements. Enel linked the purpose of its projects to competitive advantage and business improvement in order to change these perceptions.

Chr. Hansen's natural solutions for food and health challenges

Chr. Hansen is a Danish bioscience company that specialises in natural solutions for the food, beverage, nutritional, pharmaceutical and agricultural industries, supplying food cultures, probiotics, enzymes and natural colours to its customers. Thousands of microbial strains are the basis for its products.

What's striking about Chr. Hansen is the way that its business is built on addressing major global challenges. For example, it claims that if its natural microbial additives were used in all of the yoghurt in Europe, the resulting longer shelf lives would reduce wastage by 30 per cent. Good bacteria can underpin very effective alternatives to pesticides and, Chr. Hansen hopes, in creating non-genetically modified plant strains. Reducing pesticide use is topical because of recent lawsuits claiming links between well-known brands and cancer, and pesticides have been called the next asbestos by some commentators. From a dietary perspective, studies show that probiotics improve gut health and boost immune functions for humans and animals, reducing unnecessary usage of antibiotics, which is positive for global health risk management and treatment.

Chr. Hansen is creating natural solutions to take on serious environmental challenges and has been recognised by Corporate Knights for its world-leading sustainability agenda; plus its stock price has shown a strong upwards trend. Collaborations and partnerships feature strongly in its business model, with participation in dozens of national and international projects as well as tapping into associations and other platforms that support research into bacteria health, improving the documentation of probiotic strains and supporting the growth of the broader Danish biotech industry.

Yara International and the Tanzanian Growth Corridor

Shared value principles can and do play a significant role in large collective impact projects. They can induce companies to bring their business-as-usual resources to regional or systemic challenges instead of nominal community investments. Norwegian global fertiliser producer Yara International played a role in developing the Tanzanian Growth Corridor, which illustrates how shared value principles and collective impact can be linked in practice[70].

The problems Yara's products faced reaching smallholder farmers included port unloading delays, poor road infrastructure and a lack of refrigerated transport for farmers to get their crops to market unspoiled. Farmers themselves were unaccustomed to using fertiliser, had high illiteracy levels and lacked access to credit. In addition, government bans on key exports designed to protect local consumption had the unintended consequence of discouraging investment in the sector. The company worked out that there was no single intervention that would change or improve the market dynamic, so a coordinated approach was needed.

Yara worked to bring together more than 50 multinational companies, non-government organisations and government interests to form the Southern Agricultural Corridor of Tanzania with the mission of building and developing a corridor from the Indian Ocean to the western border. Funding of US$3.4 billion was sourced for physical infrastructure, better farm management practices and supporting services. Of note is the make-up of this funding, with one-third coming from government and two-thirds from the private sector. Yara's own investment of US$60 million was leveraged through the project and has boosted its sales by 50 per cent. This is a great example of a company working beyond its traditional boundaries and engaging with the entire ecosystem surrounding its business to create shared value.

Applying the new lens

There is a common theme of mutual benefit in these examples. Nestlé's oats strategy helped it address challenges that were affecting supply chain risks and costs. IAG has implemented a culture of shared value from the top down and sees strong links between those investments and its bottom line. Lion innovated by lowering alcohol concentration, and created a successful new product in a crowded and highly competitive market. Herbert Smith Freehills sees a strong business case for investments in diversity and inclusion, and CJ Korea Express helped solve last-mile delivery challenges with an inclusive delivery model. Blantyre Farms has slashed farm input costs by utilising food waste for its piggery. Chr. Hansen's entire business is predicated on major global challenges. The value proposition of Enel Green Power revolves around changes in customer preferences and a growing willingness to tackle greenhouse gas emissions through renewable power sources. Yara worked with the entire ecosystem to grow the market for its products in a way that also benefits farmers and the economy.

We will formalise the different strategy types in Chapter 7. Before we do, now that you've seen examples of shared value in action, it's worth reinforcing how it is different from philanthropic and CSR approaches.

chapter 6
beyond corporate social responsibility

Even in organisations that embrace shared value principles from the top down, it's a big task to help employees, managers, leaders and executives work out what it means for them and their day-to-day roles. It may be a completely new concept, they may have some familiarity with it or they may think it is about some slightly new form of philanthropy or CSR. I've found that the following example is very effective in helping people comprehend the differences.

Do you trust real estate agents to change the world?

If you've been to Sydney, the capital of the state of New South Wales in Australia, you may have swooned at the spectacular water views that harbour-side residents have across to the Opera House or Sydney Harbour Bridge. You may also know that property prices are very high by global standards – it's the second most expensive city in the world behind Hong Kong based on price to median household income ratios. In this part of the world, property market trends are keenly analysed and discussed at social gatherings.

Roy Morgan Research conducted a survey[71] of trust in professions and found real estate agents ranked 28th out of 30 professions in terms of perceptions of ethics and honesty. So you may find it curious that we'll be looking to the real estate profession to differentiate shared value from philanthropy and CSR. In case you're wondering, only advertisers and car salespeople ranked lower in the survey while nurses, doctors and pharmacists came out on top!

If you think about the ways in which a real estate agency can engage in a social initiative, donating to a local cause is one option. When my children were at primary school and our annual fete was looming, a local real estate agent wrote out a cheque for $200 because it had a policy of helping out schools in the area. We thanked the agency and used the money to buy books and other resources for our kids.

What could it do to take community support to the next level? It could get a staff team together to do a 50-kilometre trek and raise money for a charity, doing good and team bonding at the same time. Or help out the local high school by taking on a Year 10 student for a week of work experience. Or sponsor a local sports team, which could be partly motivated by marketing (signage and logos) and partly as a community contribution (seen to be doing the right thing). Or decide to use Forest Stewardship Council certified paper in their office printing and copying machines. All of these possible activities illustrate what a CSR agenda could look like for the business. Would any of these initiatives materially improve financial performance? Unlikely. So what might a shared value strategy look like for a real estate office?

At a forum on business and community connections, I met Eva Gerencer, who at the time was a strategic development manager for the peak body representing more than 200 not-for-profits in the Western Sydney area. Eva was presenting on a project that engaged real estate agents in the Macarthur Region in homelessness prevention, and our chance meeting led to us documenting[72] this case study using a shared value lens.

The backdrop for the initiative was a shift in government policy away from treating people who are homeless and towards the prevention of homelessness. As the peak body in the area, Eva's organisation and its members knew that they had to look for better ways to intercept people at risk. One of the pathways into homelessness is evictions from rental properties for reasons like ill health, job loss, relationship breakdown, domestic violence and mental health challenges. This often leads to couch-surfing (short-term stays on friend's lounges), living on the street or staying in refuges and hostels, all of which meet the definition of homelessness.

Here's how the project worked: they initially formed partnerships with five real estate agencies in the area (which later grew to nine). When property managers – who manage the rentals – observed a tenant falling behind in rent due to a socially driven reason, with the tenant's permission they referred them to a social services' partner who would coordinate a response. In many cases tenants weren't aware that support was available to them. In the first two years of operation, 57 tenancies were saved out of 102 referrals. The success of this project has built stronger relationships between real estate businesses and social support organisations. Ultimately, Eva's peak body hopes that the increase in understanding and trust will help reverse flows, meaning that the real estate agents and landlords will be more open to considering suitable homeless applicants for vacant rental properties in the future.

As much as we'd like to think the real estate agents are doing this purely out of the goodness of their hearts, there are business reasons why they get involved. Reducing tenancy evictions saves them hard costs, estimated at $1,000 each time an eviction is averted, and that's before factoring in soft costs such as extra management time. Furthermore, their customers (landlords) are significantly better off if an eviction is averted, saving $10,000 on average because they are not losing rent for a prolonged period of time; they avoid property remediation expenses and reletting costs. It took a while for the partnership to gain traction because the parties were not used to dealing with each other, and a defining moment came when a semi-retired agent, who could easily identify and communicate the business benefits to other agents, joined the project team.

We captured two stories in our case study. The first one comes from a real estate agent attending a routine property inspection and noticing that the female tenant was distraught due to verbal abuse from the male tenant. On returning to the office the real estate agent rang the state government's housing referral partner for advice. She then rang the female tenant and asked about her welfare and offered her a contact to talk to. The female tenant rang the housing referral partner, where the officer established that she was living in a domestic violence situation and was able to offer her a Start Safely programme subsidy. The female tenant moved away as a result of the assistance and is now safe.

In the second example, an agent rang a social sector partner about a tenant who was behind in her rent. The tenant had a serious illness and was due to go into hospital, and the landlord wanted her evicted. The government welfare agency officer rang the tenant, checked her record and found that she was not getting the correct payment due to a problem with the child support system. The problem was fixed and she was paid the arrears, her family payment was doubled and her rent assistance was increased. The officer also introduced her to a local service that helped with electricity bills. She was able to rectify the arrears situation and remain in the property.

The project has helped reduce pathways into homelessness and benefitted business at the same time, thus meeting the criteria of creating shared value. I'm sure you'll agree that this approach is more world-changing than the philanthropic or CSR programmes that the real estate agents could be undertaking. It highlights how parties within an ecosystem can work together to realise mutual gains. The important thing is that businesses become more proficient in making conscious choices about the initiatives that they choose to take on and support.

Illustrating the differences

The real estate agency example is a good one to use with someone who has never heard of shared value principles. A summary of the different corporate approaches is provided in Table 2.

Table 2: Differentiating the main forms of corporate social engagement

Approach and motivation	Form it could take	Resourcing
Shared value • Create value together • Core and profitable business	Social or environmental investments made for: • Productivity gains • Revenue growth • Transforming or innovating business models	Mobilising core assets of the business

Approach and motivation	Form it could take	Resourcing
Corporate social responsibility • Brand, reputation and licence to operate • Risk management	Programmes, accreditations or sponsorships such as: • Developmental volunteering • Critical community investments • Cause related marketing/brand enhancers • Reputation management	Limited by CSR and sponsorship budgets
Philanthropy • Corporate conscience • Right thing to do	Transactional forms of support such as: • Employee giving/ matched giving • Corporate foundation grants • Community investments • Volunteering	Donated funds, goods or other resources

Porter & Kramer's seminal shared value paper[73] and other commentaries[74] point out the contradictions and inadequacies of the CSR approach and come down hard on the notion that it's the most effective way for companies to make a difference. Companies are good at making grand pronouncements about social responsibility, but will baulk at taking action when profits are at risk. Spirited urging of companies to do the right thing will have some impact, but it's unlikely to create real change unless there is a clear business case and financial reason for doing so.

Recycling coffee cups in the staff cafeteria is far less important than, say, an industrial company reducing supply chain waste by 10 per cent. Under some responsibility-styled frameworks these two activities might be given equal weight, whereas the latter has a far greater impact. The level of materiality is important. Boosting performance and outcomes is the aim; it's not the process of picking out a social issue that isn't affecting a company and deciding to take it on.

I've also found that some people use the phrase 'shared values' instead of 'shared value', and they have very different meanings. Values are the things that you believe are important whereas value refers to benefit relative to cost. For more discussion about the types of questions that inevitably arise, please refer to the Appendix.

Now that you're more familiar with the principles, we'll take a quick look at the different strategy types.

chapter 7
unpacking strategies

Potential opportunities for creating shared value can be found any-where in your business structure. We'll now look at the three broad categories defined by Porter & Kramer before introducing you to another methodology for illustrating strategy types.

The three main strategy types

Firstly, there are the strategies labelled *reconceiving products and markets*, such as the invention of the Toyota Prius, Chr. Hansen's natural solutions or Lion's mid-strength beer. Essentially, they are about meeting current or emerging needs through innovative products or business models. The Bendigo Community Bank and Enel Green Power examples fit in here too because they're primarily about driving revenue or top-line growth.

Secondly, when social or environmental issues are imposing costs on production, there may be a business case for investing in them to lower those costs. This category is called *productivity in the value chain* because it's about doing more with less. Nestlé's Uncle Toby's oats initiative sought to reduce input costs and brand risk while increasing the reliability and quality of supply. Blantyre Farms slashed their input costs through the re-use of food waste and renewable energy generation. Marriott International's strategy was about reducing employment and turnover costs; the motivation for real estate agents to join the Macarthur Real Estate Engagement Project was reducing management time, hard costs and income loss for landlords. CJ Korea's Parcel Express strategy was about finding a lower-cost last-mile delivery solution. And Johnson & Johnson's quit smoking initiative reduced healthcare costs and increased worker productivity, returning $2.71 for every dollar invested.

The third type of strategy aims to improve the conditions of a company's ecosystem by boosting productivity, innovation or growth. It's when a company or group of companies collaborate to make investments in system-wide issues. Porter & Kramer originally called this category *enabling local cluster development*, however it's also referred to as *improving the operating environment*. When Microsoft supports the community college network it has a system-wide impact. In fact its competitors could benefit from the strategy in the same way that IAG's competitors might benefit from lower disaster recovery costs resulting from the work of the Australian Business Roundtable. Why would companies take on industry, market or regional issues that create benefits for free riders? While they could be helping competitors somewhat, they often see commercial advantages in the form of a better policy environment, supportive investments and gaining greater knowledge, data and strengthening stakeholder relationships.

A given strategy could have the features of one or more of the types described here. Yara International achieved a high rate of growth for its own products by helping to create infrastructure and systems in Tanzania. All three strategy types are present: growing revenues, reducing the cost of doing business and improving the operating environment.

Table 3 provides high-level examples of each strategy type. From a practical perspective, there's no need to be overly concerned with classifications; the important thing is that shared value principles are used, and measurement systems put in place to help determine how much value is being created.

Table 3: Examples of the three strategy types

Reconceiving products and markets	Redefining productivity in value chains	Improving the operating environment
What: Designing profitable products and services to address societal needs, including meeting the needs of under-served communities	**What:** Addressing societal problems that impose costs on the company's value chain – proactive investment may reduce those costs	**What:** Investments in improving operating conditions to boost productivity, innovation and growth – a rising tide lifts all boats!
About: Differentiation, re-positioning products or brands, creating new markets	**About:** Resource use, logistics, strengthening suppliers, distributors, employee needs, local sourcing or processing	**About:** Developing suppliers, future workforce, service providers, infrastructure, institutions or public assets

Reconceiving products and markets	Redefining productivity in value chains	Improving the operating environment
Example: Banking *Revitalising local communities by creating a community banking model, where risk and returns are shared*	**Example: Food and agriculture** *Mobile health vans to support and improve the productivity of seasonal workers*	**Example: Mining** *Local supplier and workforce development to support production efficiencies*
Example: Food and beverage *The development of innovative lower alcohol substitute products*	**Example: Legal Services** *Increasing workforce diversity to better align internal resources with client expectations and needs*	**Example: Insurance** *Influencing government policy to allow insurers to offer preventative mental health service*
Example: Property development *Including social infrastructure in new residential developments to create a new and competitive customer value proposition*	**Example: Property services** *Real estate agents partnering with community services providers to reduce preventable tenancy evictions*	**Example: Technology** *Partnering with community colleges to develop and improve the skills of the future IT workforce*

An innovation-based framework

One of the challenges with this classification system is that the form of the initiative – whether it's purely competitive, collaborative or a broader collective approach – is ultimately designed to deliver top-line growth, cost savings or both. We can categorise strategies according to their innovation features, as being incremental (small change/continuous improvement), radical (doing something fundamentally different or new) or transformational (changing the paradigm through a new business model). Several of the examples we've examined so far are shown in Diagram 3.

For example, the Nestlé oats initiative was a fundamentally new way of supporting farmers and very much weighted towards reducing costs. The strategy is about competitiveness and improving the ecosystem in which they operate. Contrast that with Yara's Tanzanian Growth Corridor that has elements of all three strategies; however it's transformative and weighted more to revenue growth.

Diagram 3: Shared value strategies viewed through an innovation lens

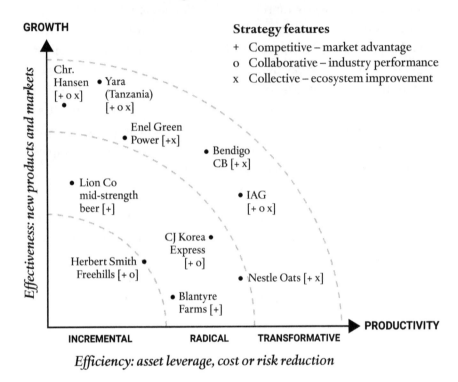

Efficiency: asset leverage, cost or risk reduction

© Phil Preston 2020

You may find this framework useful in linking shared value with your firm's innovation agenda and prioritisation process.

chapter 8

the role of government and not-for-profits

Where do government and not-for-profits fit in? Are they curious bystanders or part of the main game? What does it mean for the way they operate or form policy? They have a lot to gain from shared value strategies and can play a key role in their formation. The not-for-profit sector includes entities such as charities, community services organisations, cultural societies, associations and recreational clubs. Government includes agencies, policy-making bodies, regulators, departments and service delivery operations.

Rethinking corporate engagement for not-for-profits

Corporate engagement by not-for-profits has typically been for the purpose of gaining more funds, volunteers or other resources, by tapping into their philanthropic or CSR programme agendas. With greater curiosity emerging from not-for-profits about shared value, corporate relationship managers and CEOs are being challenged to understand what it means for their organisation and their roles. Applying shared value principles can help create deeper and more strategic forms of support from their corporate partners, however it must be put in perspective: it will rarely generate large amounts of untied cash or income unless there's a large service delivery contract component, but it will be instrumental in bringing greater non-cash resources to the table.

It may be difficult shifting to these new types of conversations, and not-for-profits will need to decide how they reconfigure their partnering efforts to make the most of their opportunities. Insurance company IAG has a ten-year partnership in place with the Australian Red Cross designed to motivate and change attitudes towards disaster preparedness. The adoption of a long timeframe is seen by both parties as a way of maximising their potential, taking the focus away from short-term programmes and towards longer-term value they can create together, especially in resilience prior to disasters. Both parties are using shared value principles to identify projects of interest.

The assets and expertise that come from the corporate side will often be the lynchpin of more strategic relationships, but that's not always the case. Australian banking and insurance company Suncorp has tapped into the distribution network of a social sector partner in rolling out insurance products designed for low-income earners[75]. According to a report into financial exclusion, one in five adults in Australia does not have general insurance cover for their car or home contents. Being on a lower income is the major cause of under-insurance, and bad luck events such as bushfire, flood, theft or accident can put a low-income earner's relatively small level of accumulated assets at risk. Suncorp partnered with not-for-profit Good Shepherd Microfinance to address the gap by creating products that cover a narrower range of insured risks compared to the higher priced and more comprehensive products in the market. For example, car theft and accident cover is available for between $4 and $9 dollars per week for insured amounts of $3,000-$5,000. For home contents, coverage of $10,000-$20,000 is available for between $5.50 and $13 dollars per week. The policy covers key items and provides for temporary accommodation costs when they are needed. It features no paperwork, an easy claims process and low excess amounts. To be eligible for these insurance products, customers must have a health care card, receive government welfare payments or have a household income under a threshold amount. For someone re-building their life post-prison release, for example, who relies on a second-hand car to get to work every day and is trying to integrate back into society, this provides an affordable insurance option.

Good Shepherd Microfinance has helped Suncorp develop this product by advocating for consumer needs – it would be risky for Suncorp to do it without a trusted partner. The product is distributed through Good Shepherd's national provider network and this low-cost distribution model makes the product economically feasible. So in this example, the main assets being leveraged are coming from the social sector partner as well as the business.

Doing more with less

Our greatest challenges are referred to as *wicked problems*, where there are so many variables and influences at play that they seem impossible to solve, such as our response to climate change or inter-generational unemployment. There are seldom any quick fixes for these types of problems and the private, public and social sectors need to work in a concerted way over many years and sometime decades to make headway. Collective impact methodology, as outlined in Chapter 2, can work well in coordinating many types of organisa-tions to tackle the root causes of these problems. Although it's hard keeping companies engaged over such long timeframes, we've seen how Nestlé, Interface and Yara International have been able to do it and create shared value. There is a middle ground or way of working that's like a hybrid approach, a cross between shared value and collective impact, where companies work effectively with governments and not-for-profits more organically to take on issues that are meaningful for all concerned.

To illustrate, I'll outline another regional project that also involves a meat processing operation. I can't explain why I've worked with several projects in this industry – it's just happened. There's a colloquial expression that Australians use to denote an area that is a long way from anywhere, "out near the back of Bourke". Bourke is a town in my adopted home state of New South Wales, and it's certainly a long way from just about everything! Getting there requires a plane trip from Sydney to Dubbo and then a four-hour drive along a very straight, flat and boring road where you have to dodge kangaroos, emus, wild goats and the odd cow along the way. The population of Bourke is just over 2,500, having declined considerably in the past two decades due to a prolonged period of drought and the closure of the cattle sale yards.

An Aboriginal employment strategy was developed out of a partnership between the community representative body, Maranguka, and the Bourke Shire Council, originating in a grassroots vision developed and endorsed by the local community. The town has historically had social and employment challenges, and this step forward was brought about by the hard work of these organisations along with the police force and other service providers. Taking the strategy forward required buy-in from all sections of the local economy, from businesses and the government to schools and residents.

The opening of a new commercial goat meat processing facility on the north side of the town is providing a strong backdrop for locals to participate in and benefit from the resulting employment opportunities. The alternative for the meat processing company would be to draw on non-locals, migrants or temporary visa holders for its workforce. Applying a shared value lens, the company appreciates that investment in developing the local workforce helps to drive down labour costs in the long run.

In the consultation process, we found that all parties – unemployed residents, community members, business owners, government operatives, school staff and not-for-profit representatives – wanted to see increased prosperity for the town and region. They each had their own way of describing what success would look and feel like. One local business owner saw "the airport re-opening" as a key indicator of success. The pharmacist said that "selling my business to a young Aboriginal family when I'm ready to retire" is his ultimate goal. Aboriginal locals focused on indicators like improved life expectancy, safety and "former students returning to high school to tell their success story". Local and state government operatives want to see reduced demand for services such as law enforcement and health; school staff want to see greater engagement from parents in their children's education, and everyone wants a safer and more vibrant main street.

After initial one-on-one consultations, we invited everyone to a session to create a plan on a page, the idea being that they would gain new perspectives from each other (the plan-on-a-page elements are described in Chapter 11). We created a safe environment for people to contribute their views, and captured the project's aims in a language that everyone could understand and agree upon. Shifting to a whole-of-community approach is hard work due to the number and complexity of the participants, however it can result in breakthroughs in terms of economic participation, community strength, big savings for government and a stronger backdrop for doing business in Bourke.

The project is now in the early implementation stage with a full-time coordinator helping to get the right processes in place to ensure that the people and organisations involved don't get distracted from their commitments. From the state government's perspective, while there is funding required for the coordinator's role, it is relatively minor compared to the amount that would be needed for an official ongoing employment programme – and when such programmes end the social benefits usually end with them. It's a sign of a maturing government approach that they are seeking to fund pathways to sustained solutions rather than ongoing programme costs. In this case, shared value principles played a role in increasing the engagement level of the meat processing company and local businesses. Government representatives were able to get the right people into the room to take our discussions forward, and the value of this enabling role shouldn't be underestimated.

Government as an enabler and facilitator

Many government departments and agencies are becoming attracted to the shared value concept because of its potential to help reduce direct outlays and the costs associated with commissioning social service providers. They are seeking to transition where possible from directly funded social interventions to enabling and facilitating partnerships between companies and not-for-profits. Government grant funding can be used to explore, trial or validate solutions, reducing the uncertainty for project partners before they make substantial investments. The Macarthur Real Estate Engagement Project that we examined in Chapter 6 benefited from a $50,000 state government development grant which was money well spent given the results it achieved. Other forms of support that governments can provide include policy change, supportive regulation, tax incentives, and procurement and grant-making preferences.

Regulation is not necessarily bad for companies as it can assist them in capitalising on shared value solutions. In the 1980s it became clear that chemicals such as chlorofluorocarbons (CFCs) were depleting the ozone layer and Du Pont, deciding that making CFCs was no longer a sustainable business, backed the proposed regulation. Although the decision was assisted by moral and ethical influences from within the company, Du Pont also saw an advantage in positioning itself as a major provider of alternative or substitute products. Scientists are now observing[76] a gradual healing in the ozone layer, which has resulted from a combination of commercial incentives and supportive regulation.

A similar dynamic was at play for Australian residential property developer, Stockland. When its CEO, Matthew Quinn, was faced with legislation requiring more expensive insulation for new homes, he saw it as an opportunity to lead the market in the new regulatory regime. The change of stance opened up a raft of new and innovative thinking[77] including the pre-funding of social infrastructure such as childcare facilities and new schools in residential developments. Normally these assets wouldn't be added until later in the development cycle, so why fund them earlier on? Stockland had created a liveability index to help inform the link between these features and product pricing points, and was able to make the business case for including them (or not). It found that earlier inclusion increased the attractiveness, demand and pricing points for the dwellings. Delivering greater social benefits has also led to shorter development approval times from government authorities, thus reducing financing costs.

Private industry can do some of the heavy lifting for government, especially in areas that are relevant to market needs or competitiveness.

Government can then better focus its efforts on what it does best (policy and administration), and it could free up monies to support those societal challenges that have much less market relevance and are unlikely to attract interest from the corporate sector.

Focal points for government

There are three key areas I'd recommend government and their departments should consider when getting started:

1. Interdependence

This is about mindset. Reflect on the interdependence rather than independence between business and society, and encourage cross-sector collaborations with shared value features. Government representatives can help in identifying opportunities and curating forums to develop them. Many of the government clients I've worked with realise that isolated interventions – where not-for-profits deliver programmes independently of other initiatives – aren't always effective nor can they be sustained without substantial ongoing, committed funding. Bringing business to the table in a sustained way brings great benefits.

2. Risk-taking

The terms 'government' and 'risk-taking' are seldom synonymous. However there are two types of risks: reckless, uninformed risks to be avoided, and calculated risks based on informed assessments, which are warranted. A government representative I've worked with on the employment challenges in Wagga Wagga, Donna Argus, has relentlessly pursued taking calculated risks in pushing for greater collaboration between local industry, government departments and social service providers. She has been willing to question the status quo and push for greater accountability. For example, when there's been concern expressed that our process might be "setting youths up to fail", Donna has challenged it with the counter view of "if we don't do it, we may be preventing them from succeeding." Her approach has led to new and smarter ways of working together, and many companies in the area are now collaborating on solutions to social challenges independently of formal project processes. That's about as good as it gets from a government perspective.

The companies we've been dealing with have also been pushed into thinking outside the square, and Donna has been there to test the boundaries of what can be achieved. It is a difficult role to play and she is one of the government sector champions who has embraced shared value principles to bring the private sector to the table in solving complex problems.

3. Capacity building

As is the case in the for-profit and not-for-profit sectors, building the right skills within government is necessary if it is to play an effective role. Firstly, around the conceptual and technical aspects of bringing projects to life and, secondly, constantly reviewing the landscape through a shared value lens to find, develop and enhance opportunities. Exactly where such roles sit depends on the structure of the departments in question and the scope of their policy and operations. For example, in local government these skills typically span the economic and community development roles.

Complex multi-sector partnerships

JP Morgan Chase & Co has been lauded[78] for its work in revitalising down and out neighbourhoods in Detroit. It's an example of shared value playing a role in a bigger collective impact project, with many different organisations coming together to tackle the same problem. For its part, JP Morgan Chase & Co draws on its philanthropic social responsibility and business innovation (i.e. shared value) agendas in collaborating with many government departments and not-for-profits. Invest Detroit is the financing platform that supports business expansion, real estate development, the creation and retention of jobs and the revitalisation of distressed areas[79]. It has committed US$150 million to help finance critical elements of the economic recovery project such as career training, technical education and capital for small local businesses. It also focuses on more specific areas of social need, including new types of job skills, providing the capital and expertise that women and minority entrepreneurs need to grow their businesses, investing in locally driven projects for improving distressed neighbourhoods and helping families build stronger financial futures. The firm leverages the expertise of its employees through its own volunteering programme, and analyses data to maximise the impact of investments.

Based on this work, a scaled up version known as the AdvancingCities Initiative[80] is being deployed in other parts of the US with a pool of US$500 million, half philanthropic monies and half from an investment fund providing low-cost, long-term capital. From the experience in Detroit, contributions are expected to leverage an additional US$1 billion in capital. The key point is that AdvancingCities is not doing this on its own: the model relies on collaborations with local civic, community and business leaders. The overall strategy is predicated on the interplay between jobs, housing and economic progress. The CEO, Jamie Dimon, notes that you need skills to get a job and a job provides housing, and also that if they don't have housing then people can't get or maintain jobs. Shared value principles have played a key role in mobilising resources for community gains.

There are tremendous opportunities for governments and not-for-profits to work with companies using shared value principles to do far more than they can on their own.

+ + +

Now that we've differentiated shared value in action from philanthropy and CSR and looked at examples, how can you apply these same principles for the benefit of your company or organisation?

SECTION III
finding your opportunities

Companies are good at coordinating complex activities to produce financial returns. Not-for-profits are good at starting with limited resources and maximising their impact in society. These are two very different capabilities, and to create shared value you'll need a healthy mix of commercial acumen and social impact skills. Plus, you will be collaborating with business partners and stakeholders that you've rarely dealt with before, so you'll need methods and tools for unearthing great ideas, evaluating them and developing a business case. If you're doing it well, it should look very much like your normal innovation process with some enhancements. Your commercial aims are the same; it's just that a societal challenge is the spark or driving force. In this section you'll be introduced to methods for unearthing and developing opportunities.

chapter 9
mindset: your ticket to play

Is your glass half empty or half full? The answer to this question is your own interpretation. Likewise in business, a glass half full approach looks for the innovation potential in problems. Applying shared value principles requires the same mindset shift: seeing problems as potential opportunities.

Who's helping who?

The chart (Diagram 4) showing the intersection between business and societal needs is very much like a partnering proposition, where you ask "Who has what I need and who needs what I have?" You may have resources and skills that others need and they may be able to help you too. There are two main ways to start: one is to focus on your business agenda and look for areas where societal challenges are holding you back or offering new opportunities. The second is to scan the problems prevalent in your region, industry or market to see which ones intersect with your business agenda, and then figure out if there is a business case for investing in them. You should have your radar tuned to both of these methods plus another three that I'll outline shortly.

Diagram 4: The intersection of business and societal goals

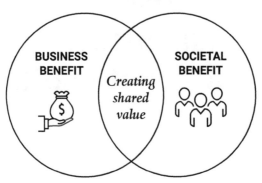

Once you do lock onto the issues that you think present opportunities, your next task will be to prioritise the best ones and start sketching them out, asking questions like who benefits from this and how? What commercial benefits are we seeking? Whom do we need to work with to design and implement them? What are the key assumptions or risks we will need to address in building a business case?

Before embarking on any of these processes, the right foundations need to be in place, and that's all about mindset.

Mindset shifts

The main shift in thinking is the one from independence to interdependence as we discussed earlier, moving away from a mentality of profit first and social support second to one where the latter also drives the former. They reinforce each other. Intuitively it makes sense that a business can only be successful in the long run if it is addressing the genuine needs of its customers and the communities it works in. Your first task is to ensure that the important decision-makers and people around you have this mindset. Focusing purely on sales growth or cost reductions for the sake of short-term gains may keep your shareholders happy for a while, but it also increases the risk that sooner or later you'll fall out of step with market preferences or needs, and that may have far-reaching consequences.

Lion has found the language of shared value to be effective[81,82] in illustrating the link between profit and purpose for its staff, whom it encourages to consider what they can do in their day jobs to implement these principles. Lion has found three key elements in nurturing[83] a shared value culture: firstly, setting out its organisational purpose[84] as "championing sociability and helping people to live well" and placing that at the heart of everything it does. Secondly, focusing on the current and future needs of society and, thirdly, establishing recruitment and management practices that ensure people coming into the organisation have this mindset. This is an excellent template to follow, but I would add a word of caution: the language you use within your organisation plays a critical role, so think very carefully as to whether you want to explicitly introduce the term "shared value" to your workforce. In executive and leadership conversations it may sit well, however it can be confusing for people right across organisations if you're not going to invest in educating everyone in its finer points. Quite often your people just need to be clear about your true business purpose, how that connects to their role, and that they have scope to innovate based upon it.

To help educate your people in the mindset shift, you can start by outlining the differences between philanthropy, corporate social responsibility and shared value, referring to the examples and tables in Section II. You can invite not-for-profit representatives to talk about the challenges that they and their clients face or, even better, go and meet them onsite – that helps fill out the picture of what they do and why, and will likely highlight how it's all done with very scarce resources. Debrief regularly though to identify if shared value principles are playing a role, or see if you can come up with ideas about how they may be utilised in creating greater impact.

Another interesting insight into the qualities needed comes from Cemex, a Mexican based building products company, which made a public declaration of ignorance[85] to signal its intention to better understand the needs of the low-income earner market. That led to a raft of ideas and the creation of new financing models, products and support services which cut home renovation times and costs by two-thirds while also empowering local suppliers and tradespeople. Even as Cemex struggled after the global financial downturn of 2008, its lower-income market products remained profitable. The mindset that's needed is aided by the qualities of curiosity, empathy and humility as demonstrated by Cemex.

For a personal perspective on mindset change, soon after I left my corporate career with the aim of somehow getting involved in addressing community challenges, I met with Jenny Briscoe-Hough, head of the Port Kembla Community Project situated in the heavily industrial southern suburbs of Wollongong, an hour's drive south of Sydney. Port Kembla came into being when the ready availability of coal attracted the copper and steel industries, peaking in the 1920s and subsequently declining slowly. Waves of migrants from all over the world arrived after World War II, in the 1950s and '60s, seeking employment and a new life. As a haven for the working classes, it's a suburb that has historically done it tough and still has its share of health and welfare issues to contend with. Based on unemployment levels and prison and psychiatric admissions, it is one of the most disadvantaged areas in the state of New South Wales. Despite being 'statistically poor', there is a strong undercurrent of positivity – it feels more vibrant and connected than many places.

Jenny and her team are based in the local community centre, and I have to admit I was fairly naive and overconfident when we first met, expecting that the problems in her community could be solved with some of my extra thinking on board. Instead, those 90 minutes transformed my life. I realised I was way out of my depth when hearing about the day-to-day challenges and the lives of people in this area. Jenny told me about deep-seated unemployment problems, young women dealing with domestic violence, drug and alcohol abuse and a raft of health and other problems. Up until then, I had thought solving homelessness was about providing people with housing. The reality is that there's a set of intertwined problems that needs managing, like substance abuse, domestic violence, family pressures, physical health, mental health and literacy. Despite the daily challenges in her area, Jenny and her team have chalked up many successes. One of her projects is a not-for-profit (social enterprise) funeral business called Tender Funerals that's been operating very successfully for over three years. It provides affordable, culturally sensitive and environmentally friendly funeral options for their diverse community – options that aren't provided by mainstream funeral operators, and at much lower price points.

What I learned from that first visit was that I had little comprehension of the social problems that exist at grass roots level, and no idea how complex and connected they are. I hadn't realised that it takes years and often decades to create meaningful and positive social change. It helps to know what you don't know and gaining new perspectives is a good place to start. It's a reminder that short-term thinking and actions aren't going to solve our deep-seated issues. If we are fixated with company quarterly earnings, we are a long way from having the wherewithal and patience to participate in this revolution. Our mindset must be right.

Expanding our view of 'the system'

Another shift we've discussed is from creating *business systems* to proactively working across entire *ecosystems*. To do this, I'd highly recommend engaging with a greater variety of organisations and inquiring about their challenges and needs. CJ Korea Express engaged with the Ministry of Health & Welfare and several municipal governments in its seniors parcel delivery strategy. Insurance company IAG engages with social enterprises and grass roots community organisations to better inform its understanding of social resilience. Reaching out to wider stakeholder groups is a common theme in JP Morgan Chase & Co's Invest Detroit initiative and Yara International's role in transforming Tanzanian agriculture.

Another good example[86] of cultivating ecosystems comes from the mining industry, where local supply chain development has proven to be commercially smart. In Mozambique, the government mandates strict targets in local supplier and workforce content. Petroleum and gas exploration company Anadarko finds that the policy has good intentions, but the capacity of local business to deliver is often very limited. Its response is to work with not-for-profit partner Pyxera in developing local providers at the beginning of projects, before the regulated requirements come into effect. Operationally, they benefit from a supplier base that has a far greater capacity to deliver their project needs. At a higher level, this builds trust between the company and government, which in turn opens up new opportunities. This same conceptual model can be adapted to different types of projects. A subsidiary of Rio Tinto – Pacific Aluminium's Bell Bay processing plant in Tasmania – helped build the capacity of local engineering suppliers so they could be more competitive when bidding for maintenance contracts against offshore companies. In one instance, a local firm successfully tendered for a multi-million dollar supply agreement and hired new employees – a significant outcome for an area that's had ongoing workforce cutbacks.

We must acknowledge the brutal truth that it is hard for a business to trade off short-term financial returns for greater, long-term value unless it has a strong and purposeful culture, well thought through incentive structures and good reason to believe that it will work. Shifting the dial requires change on many fronts and mindset is where it must start. A summary of the key mindset shifts is outlined in Table 4 and, along with the examples presented in this book, you may find it a useful checklist when you start applying the principles yourself.

Table 4: The essential mindset shifts

Shift from...	... to	Explanation
Independence	Interdependence	Acknowledging your success is linked to the success of those around you.
Business systems	Ecosystems	Going beyond your traditional value chain to working collaboratively with new partners and stakeholders in the ecosystem surrounding you.
Funded programmes	New business models	Shifting away from narrowly focused and expensive social interventions to new business models that create self-sustaining solutions.

Shift from...	... to	Explanation
Internal development	Co-designing solutions	From internally generating solutions to co-designing solutions with partners.
Commanding and controlling	Influencing and empowering	From directly controlling all aspects of your projects to working with a range of interests and agendas.
CSR department programmes	Business-as-usual	Initiatives are driven by core strategic and operational needs rather than the CSR department.
Risk management and compliance	Value creation	Looking beyond brand enhancement, reputation risk and preserving licence to operate to creating value together.
Passive	Proactive	These initiatives won't find you; you have to do some exploring and testing to make them happen.
Short term results	Patient investments	From fuelling short-term returns to longer-term, value-adding investments.

It is possible for subsets of people or teams within your organisation to have the right mindset and apply shared value principles without your whole organisation being on board. The upside is that you have scope to develop your own breakthroughs, but the downside is that your work may not be as well understood nor supported up the line. Companies leading in this field have found it's important to differentiate shared value projects and initiatives from capacity building activities, such as internal education, to creating the right environment for them to flourish. Nicola Robins, a South African-based shared value practitioner has observed there are three stages of organisational maturity when it comes to applying the principles. The first level is where your organisation is starting out and may be running education sessions or ideation workshops to find opportunities. The second stage is where you and your partners are able to develop and implement opportunities with greater speed. And the third level is when the skills and processes are deeply embedded across your organisation.

Another feature of the mindset of leading companies in this space is the outspoken nature of their executives and the way they articulate their rationale for applying the principles. The CEO of life insurer AIA Australia, Damien Mu, saw mental health-related claims rising rapidly[87] from 13 per cent to 25-30 per cent of total claims from one year to the next. His response has been to support staff in their work-life balance and encourage clients to become healthier through insurance premium reduction incentives. At a more systemic level AIA Australia is pushing for legislative change in the care that life insurers can provide for mental health prevention. The current legislation prohibits insurers paying for early intervention measures – they can only provide support once someone's condition has worsened. Damien is a pragmatist, noting that 'purpose' sounds pretty cool when you hear it in a TED talk, whereas it takes a much higher level of care to go ahead and effect positive change.

Review the shifts in Table 4 and gauge where your organisation is at – in part or as a whole. If you find the features listed in the first column are dominating, you have some work to do in creating buy-in for this new way of thinking. In all of the examples we've sketched out so far, the right mindset has allowed the discovery of new possibilities. Take the onus away from your CSR agenda and aim at business-as-usual practices. It's your ticket to play.

chapter 10
identifying your opportunities

Innovation is change that adds value. Exactly where your opportunities lie is hard to predict in advance and there are no hard and fast rules about the best or worst ways of generating great ideas. Some processes tend to work better than others, and we'll look at a visual representation of shared value strategy components before unpacking five methods to help you start exploring.

The innovation process

There's no magic wand for innovation; even the best ideas require creativity and support. To illustrate, Becton Dickinson (BD) manufactures and sells medical devices and is valued at more than US$65 billion on the stock market. A significant proportion of its revenues comes from safety syringes, devices created in response to needle stick injuries, potential transmissions of the HIV virus and other infections to health workers. Responding to journal articles about these problems, evidence in the form of injury data and advocacy from unions, BD developed and introduced the first safety syringe[88] in 1988. Revenues grew from US$5 million per annum to more than US$2 billion by 2012, representing its largest single product and amounting to a quarter of company sales. It cut injuries to nurses by half in the period from 1993 to 2004 alone. So, how did this innovation come about? And how was the opportunity captured?

An internal team at BD developed the idea[89] based on their personal interest in the problem. The CEO and board supported the idea when they realised there was a far bigger opportunity. An invention alone doesn't make for world-changing results; it has to be complemented by the right type of organisational assets and support processes. In this case, there were investments of billions of dollars to build up manufacturing capacity. Healthcare worker safety was an attractive growth segment and implementing the strategy required extensive engagement with healthcare facilities and frontline workers. BD also had to provide resources to motivate the uptake and proper use of the new devices, which required a range of partnerships to raise awareness, influence policy and deliver training programmes. BD was able to make the most of this opportunity by virtue of its proactive mindset and organisational maturity. The fact that it came about as a response to a social issue – worker injuries – is what brings it into the shared value realm. The safety syringe systems were developed as part of core business, not a standalone CSR programme, and required patient investment. The path followed ticks the mindset requirements and transformations outlined earlier.

A shared value strategy can be visually represented using the format shown in Diagram 5, comprising the intersection of a societal challenge, a business opportunity and the assets being leveraged to make it work. For example, Bendigo and Adelaide Bank leveraged their banking expertise, systems and infrastructure in establishing their community banking model, and on the community side they relied upon the strength of local networks and financial capacity.

In Chapter 8 we saw how Good Shepherd Microfinance's national distribution network was vital to the development of Suncorp's low income earner insurance products, without which the distribution costs would have been too high and the product would not have been feasible.

**Diagram 5: The three core components
of a shared value strategy**

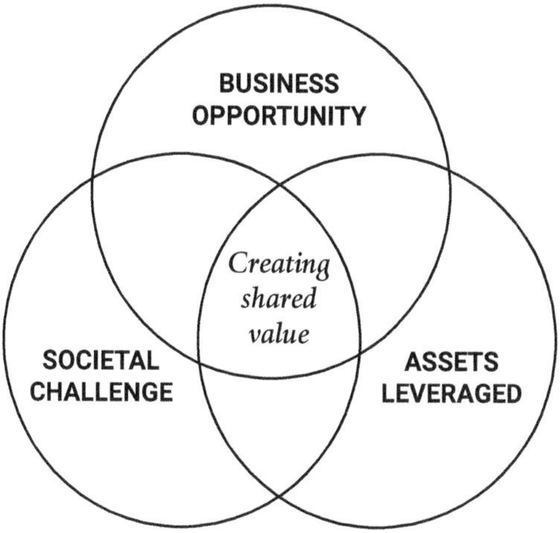

Source: Porter & Kramer

It's worth mapping your own assets and strengths, highlighting the ones that are quite outstanding or underutilised, those that are in demand and those carrying a high value in the market place. External perspectives may be useful for you too if this is a process you haven't gone through before – people outside of your organisation may see key assets and strengths that you don't. In the Becton Dickinson example, the assets included the people (human capital) who came up with the idea and the company's ability to design, fund investment, form partnerships and scale up the product. A better understanding of your own key assets will be useful background information to have by your side as you work through the five methods.

Method 1: Portfolio review

In educational or working sessions on shared value, a useful exercise is to ask people to think of a social initiative that they are familiar with – either involving their organisation or another – and work out where it sits on the X-Y chart shown in Diagram 6. That helps crystallise their thoughts around the level of impact and scale being achieved.

Diagram 6: Plot your portfolio of social initiatives

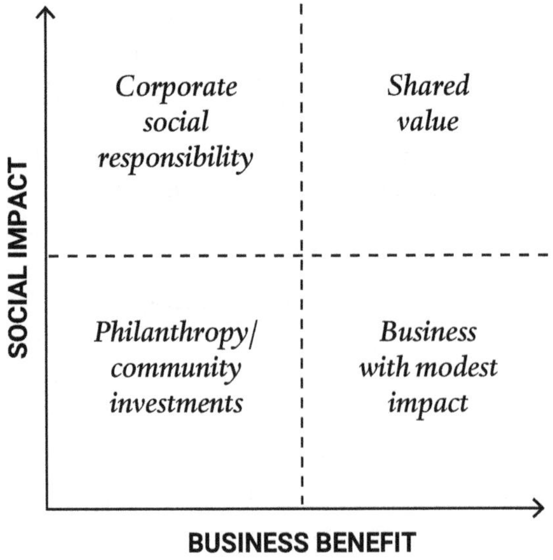

Source: Derived from Porter & Kramer

For example, when Kimberly-Clark Australia & New Zealand, the owner of a leading nappy/diaper brand, sponsors a children's hospital foundation it provides products free of charge to help in the care of sick kids. The level of social impact may be low to mid-axis, because it is helpful but not game-changing in terms of social impact. The company is motivated by brand and reputation and there is little in the way of new value creation for them, so their initiative would sit in the philanthropy/community investment zone. Becton Dickinson's safety syringes, on the other hand, would be in the top-right quadrant because of the link between significant injury reduction and profitability.

Some initiatives may start out as philanthropic or CSR programmes and move into the shared value zone. Becton Dickinson could have stationed its safer injection ideas in its CSR department, assigning a small budget and doing its best. Instead, it saw the potential to catapult the initiative from the CSR quadrant and into the shared value zone. But if you are in the shared value zone, don't expect to stay there forever. There may be competitive responses over time that reduce the size of your gains. Lion's XXXX Gold mid-strength beer was embraced by consumers when it was first launched, but in time other brands started crowding out that space. The value captured declined as competitors caught up. This is the reality of any corporate innovation cycle, where your initiatives may deliver exceptional value in the early years before returns start normalising. However, we did note earlier that it's much harder to copy a business model and the relationships associated with it than it is to copy a product.

Plotting all of your existing social and environmental initiatives on this X-Y chart is a good place to start. Not only does that neatly capture the characteristics of your current portfolio, but by applying a shared value lens you may see the potential for some of your initiatives to create significantly more value. In fact, you may already be in the shared value zone without realising it, or you may have initiatives that you think are creating shared value but don't have the metrics or measurement systems to prove it, so measurement may become your immediate action item. You may find all your existing initiatives clustered in the lower impact areas, prompting discussions about reshaping or rationalising your portfolio. You should ask questions like:

- Is this what we want our portfolio to look like?

- Are there biases or clusters in certain areas?

- Which ones are essential from a community, branding or reputation perspective?

- How many of them benefit our core business and bottom line?

- Could any of our resources be better deployed elsewhere?

- Have we gained insights to help us identify shared value opportunities?

- Which prospective partners can help us develop our ideas?

There's a trend for major corporations to conduct these types of reviews, meaning that not-for-profits may be increasingly challenged to retain existing sponsorships in their current form. The X-Y chart exercise is also valuable for not-for-profits in mapping the characteristics of their corporate partnerships, with the aim of making similar choices about how they want them to look in the future. Bringing business to the table can be hard work and there may be a sense of inequity or power imbalance in partnerships. I always encourage not-for-profits to brainstorm as many potential shared value ideas as they can before testing the market because, no matter how good any one idea may be, it may not suit their ideal corporate partner at a given point in time for a multitude of reasons.

Portfolio review is a good place to start. Even if it doesn't lead to great new ideas, it does help in familiarising your colleagues with the shared value concept and the aims of your innovation process.

Method 2: Business opportunities

Every part of your business can be put under the spotlight. Tools like the *Business Model Canvas*[90] are useful to map out your business structure from production though to sales and after-market servicing. The challenge is to find and lock onto your best ideas, and put your precious time and resources into developing them.

Consider workforce issues. A consulting firm may notice several staff or partners take extended leave due to mental health problems and question whether it could invest in better prevention and management strategies to improve wellbeing, productivity and retention. It may already have an affiliation with a mental health charity that could provide a good sounding board. Or be able to talk to its superannuation/pension fund insurer to obtain insights, or join the supportive programmes it runs. A manufacturing or logistics company may notice that staff absences in supplier companies, such as contracted delivery services, are constraining its own ability to meet customer service levels. In probing the causes of those absences it finds physical health, mental health and relationship breakdowns are key, and starts exploring the business case for working with suppliers on better prevention and management.

Sometimes the opportunities are fairly obvious and the challenge is more around making the business case and implementation. When they are not so obvious, you'll spend more time in the creative zone before you're able to start the development process. Table 5 provides a default set of questions you can use to start teasing out ideas, but don't fall into the trap of assuming this is just a conversation to have with your high-level leaders and executives. You'll be well served to engage with frontline employees, operational staff, business partners, customers, government, regulators and other stakeholders to gain their unique perspectives and insights to inform your discovery process.

Table 5: Probing questions for business opportunities

Questions for business
What's holding back the development of our markets, industry or region, and which of those issues are societal challenges that we could take on using a business case?
What are our own top five strategic or operational challenges and which ones intersect with social or environmental issues?
Are there societal issues or trends that present new product or market opportunities?
Can we gain a performance edge over our competitors by tackling certain societal problems?
What social or environmental issues are affecting our customers that we could help them with?
Are societal factors constraining the performance of our operations, suppliers or distributors?
Are there issues inhibiting the productivity and performance of our workforce?
Is the local labour market sufficiently developed to support our current and future workforce?
Could we improve our business model or profitability through innovative, social sector partnerships?
Can we derive more value from our existing social sector partnerships or relationships?
What knowledge, skills or resources do we possess that not-for-profits would value highly?
What do not-for-profits and government agencies possess that is of great value to our business?

We've already looked at some of the dilemmas companies face when creating their strategies, such as weighing up the nutritional quality of ice cream versus the responsible sourcing of ingredients. It's likely you'll need input from partners, stakeholders and independent advisers as to the efficacy of the benefits you're creating. Several companies have established independent advisory groups to test their ideas across a wide range of views and interests.

Uber provides an illustration of the complexity of social factors, having disrupted the taxi industry through its informal network of private cars and drivers. Drivers can earn money without having to buy an expensive taxi plate or plates, and customers report that they enjoy the service quality and demand-based pricing structure. In theory, there are environmental benefits from greater utilisation of existing transport assets. On the flip side, however, many Australian taxi plate owners have seen the value of their taxi plates plunge, leading to financial hardship and suicides[91], matching similar experiences overseas. Critics claim that Uber has bullied its way into new markets by deliberately breaking regulations, gaining a hard-to-dislodge foothold as regulators struggled or weren't willing to level the playing field for competition. The social trade-offs have not been great – this has cost lives.

I hope you aren't faced with such unattractive or stark options. The main advice I can give is to be aware of all the meaningful positive and negative impacts (externalities) embedded in your strategies, make conscious choices about what you do and don't do, and communicate your rationale in an open and honest way.

Method 3. Starting from the social side

Another approach is to start with prevalent social or environmental issues and review your business, industry and markets from this perspective. The United Nations Sustainable Development Goals[92] (first mentioned in Chapter 4) provide a good framework for performing this analysis, especially if your business footprint is large or spans many countries. The goals relate to 17 categories of global challenges and are further broken down into 169 sub-goals. For example, goals 2 (zero hunger), 3 (good health and wellbeing) and 12 (responsible consumption and production) are Chr. Hansen's main focus areas. Enel Green Energy is primarily tackling goal 7 (affordable and clean energy) and goal 13 (climate action). Herbert Smith Freehill's workforce diversity and inclusion strategy is partly aligned to goal 5 (gender equality).

Once you're familiar with the high level SDGs, start brainstorming shared value opportunities by asking:

- Which categories and sub-categories are most relevant to our industry?

- Which ones cross over with our corporate purpose?

- Which of these issues do we see playing out in our region?

- Which ones intersect with our strategic priorities?

- Where might the greatest payoffs lie?

- What types of partnerships would be required to gain expertise, mitigate trust issues or to explore and develop ideas further?

A few years ago I stumbled across a good example of how an innovative business model came together for a retailer with inspiration from an environmental challenge[93]. Greg Leslie is the licensee of the Battery World store in Townsville (Queensland, Australia), a retail franchise selling car batteries and other portable power devices. Greg acquired the Townsville licence and re-opened a store that had been closed for four months. He recalls how it was a very busy and crazy time because it coincided with him and his wife having triplets! The business was competing against several other car battery sellers on the town's auto strip and he was finding it hard to differentiate his offering from theirs, plus there was a degree of brand damage from the store's recent closure. So how did he change the game and propel his store from a poor performer to become the top performer in the country?

Apart from being a savvy business operator, Greg is passionate about the environment. He thought a recycling initiative that engaged local schools might hold the key because young kids tend to care about the environment, but often lack the means to get involved or feel empowered to make a difference. He set up a household battery recycling service, putting special bins in his own store as well as in participating schools, where household batteries could be dropped off free of charge. He spoke at school assemblies and provided educational materials about recycling for teachers to complement their science programmes. Greg had to collect and then pay for the batteries to be disposed of properly, however the upside came from schoolchildren urging their parents to drop off any additional used batteries at his store. Local political figures were keen to be associated with his initiative so he gained a great deal of free, third-party endorsement in the media. Foot traffic increased in Greg's store and he recorded 20 per cent rolling annual sales growth for the following two years.

Looking in from the outside, his strategy may have seemed foolish because it was costing him money to properly dispose of the batteries. However, thanks to the advocacy of schoolchildren to their parents and the raft of positive media, foot traffic increased and converted into sales, more than offsetting the disposal costs. Within two and a half years of acquiring the licence, Greg became the top performer out of 70 stores in the country and, as a result, a base level of recycling (bins in store) was embedded across the national network with ready-made programmes available for the larger stores to roll out in schools. His local government area benefitted from lower levels of contaminated waste and reduced recovery costs. After the bins were added to the entire Battery World network, the franchise as a whole was recycling 36 tonnes of household batteries per annum. Competitors weren't responding because they either didn't understand the value created or lacked the motivation or means. This shows how, even for this relatively small business, the profit motive can drive social or environmental outcomes. Greg knew the issue he wanted to target and created a strategy around it.

Method 4. Purpose driven

Purpose is very powerful for embedding the right mindset and a culture of shared value across a company. Recall that Bendigo and Adelaide Bank describes its purpose as "seeking to feed into prosperity and not off of it". This provides an anchor for its ongoing relevance to customers and an ethos for the way it does business. Chr. Hansen expresses its purpose as "improving food and health" and the three pillars it adopts are food cultures, plant protection and health and wellbeing. And in Chapter 2 we saw how Pearson adapted its purpose to "helping people make progress in their lives through learning".

The current trend is for purpose to move from the periphery of business to the core. A study[94] of 28 high growth companies across the US, Europe and India found those companies drew on purpose to think more broadly about business opportunities rather than feeling limited by their existing playing field. An example is "a better world for pets" adopted by Mars Petcare that has driven the acquisition of veterinary services, taking them beyond products and into services. Another example is the Swedish security company Securitas that has traditionally sold physical man-hours. In pursuing its purpose of "contributing to a safer society", it has bundled up physical guarding, electronic security and risk management to create new offerings, strengthen relationships with clients and increase profitability.

We noted back in Chapter 5 the purpose of insurance company IAG is "we make your world a safer place". That conveys the value proposition presented to customers. Chairperson Elizabeth Bryan notes[95] that "If you're confused about your purpose it's hard to do anything". She says it requires authenticity, passion and commitment to instil a renewed purpose across an organisation, and don't bother trying if you're not prepared to give it 100 per cent. It's about building the consideration of your purpose into everything you do. We also noted how it doesn't say anything about insurance – giving licence to explore adjacent product and market opportunities. IAG has further broken down its purpose into three pillars: safer, stronger and more confident communities. Creating pillars is an approach that leading companies are using to convert their overarching purpose into a more tangible set of themes and these features may evolve over time. Note how IAG and Securitas have a similar purpose despite being in very different industries – food for thought.

In the book *Tribal Leadership*, authors Logan, King and Fischer-Wright explain how they examined the traits of serially high-performing companies, and found they are predominately those where employees see themselves as part of a team delivering results for a noble cause. They found that companies pursuing a social mission are often more powerful than those focusing on their competition, adding weight to the idea that purpose provides a strong platform for outperformance. We've looked at how IAG has shifted its emphasis from selling insurance to *making your world a safer place*. Similar shifts are going on in well-known companies such as Nike (from shoes to health and wellness), IBM (from computing to smart cities), BASF (from chemicals to enabling life), and so on. In many cases they are redefining their reason for existence from an activity to an outcome. As noted earlier with respect to Pearson's journey, a clear purpose alone does not create transformational performance. Nokia was so immersed in executing its strategy[96] that it was unable to fulfil its stated purpose of connecting people.

Purpose is becoming serious business. The advent of Hurricane Katrina caused Walmart to question its purpose[97] and how it can better help society. As a first responder to the natural disaster, it played a vital role in getting life-saving goods to people in need. The CEO at the time, Lee Scott, put the idea to the leadership team that they could be that kind of company every day. The team set big goals such as being powered by 100 per cent renewable energy and producing zero waste. Updates to those goals have seen the inclusion of three more objectives: retail workforce development, using procurement as a way of supporting disadvantaged groups and pushing for sustainable practices throughout their entire supply chain. Walmart presently sells guns, and with more and more mass shootings in the US they have been drawn into the gun control debate, tightening ammunition sales and dissuading customers from openly carrying guns in stores.

As a fourth avenue for creating shared value, you may want to review your corporate purpose and open up conversations about its relevance and effectiveness, evaluating in particular whether it is conveying an activity, business goal or a societal benefit. It could be the launching pad for a raft of new and innovative ideas that move your business forward with strong buy-in from your workforce and customers.

Method 5. Process integration

As a fifth and final method, this is a logical extension of everything we've looked at thus far, where the challenge is to integrate shared value principles into all the things you already do. Given that it's about bringing the societal agenda into core business, integration makes sense. At a minimum, you can add some extra questions to enhance your existing business processes – there's no need to fundamentally change or replace them. For example, in your new product development processes, why not scan for the wider set of problems your customers may be facing? Why not include a conversation about shared value as it relates to policy, processes and practices in your strategy off-site days? Or formalise the way in which you gather insights from your frontline staff? In other words, use this lens to make enhancements across your entire business.

A good example of integration comes from a property management company that has a problem asset: a shopping centre where the number of security incidents is high. When the team told me how many incidents were occurring I remember thinking it was a high monthly rate... until they informed me that it was their daily number! They recognise they have an incentive to address the underlying causes of these social disruptions. They're also realistic and know that it will be a long and challenging process. If they can fix the problem, people will feel safer, the shopping experience will be much improved, turnover will increase and the centre's valuation will rise. However, what impresses me most is that the task of rectifying the situation is reflected in the CEO's personal performance goals. It's a great way of operationalising their intent by integrating their desire to create a solution into the executive's performance metrics.

The takeaway is that you don't need to fundamentally change anything or set up a shared value team – you can apply the lens to enhance everything you currently do.

How will you identify your opportunities?

There are more ways of seeking out shared value ideas and opportunities than I've shown here, such as reviewing literature or case studies, but the five methods outlined above provide you with more than enough ideas to get started. I strongly suggest that you seek input from people right across your organisation and consider forming cross-functional teams to start shaping and honing them, with senior leaders and executives reviewing and helping to prioritise the best ones. Advisory or steering groups are helpful as you start moving from concepts to developing and designing solutions, and in gaining perspectives outside your immediate realm.

chapter 11
development and implementation tips

Once you've been brainstorming and come up with a potpourri of ideas, which ones should you focus on? How do you take them forward in an efficient and effective way? The goal is to focus on the ideas that are most likely to deliver value and we'll look at how you can prioritise and map them out, along with tips for making the business case as well as a discussion about measurement.

Prioritising your ideas

Before getting too excited by specific ideas – or even before you start exploring ideas at all – it's worth devising the criteria you'll use for making your assessments. In Table 6, there's a menu of items that serves as a starting point that you can add to or modify according to your own situation or priorities. It helps you think through what's important in advance. One company I work with has "potential for scalability" high on their priority list, which is a way of saying that they prefer a smaller number of higher impact initiatives to a larger number of lower impact ones. Such an approach shows confidence in their ability to find, develop and implement shared value strategies. It suits them, but may not suit everyone.

Table 6: Items for possible inclusion in your criteria

Criteria	Question to be asked
Context	Does this make sense for us given our purpose, mission, strategic agenda and operating environment?
Materiality	Are the business and societal benefits relative to the estimated costs of producing them significant and likely to be in the shared value zone?
Confidence	At this point in time, how confident are we that the above benefits can be realised? Can we firm up our underlying assumptions quickly and easily?
Priority	If we could implement all of our ideas, where would this one sit in the pecking order?
Urgency	To what extent is speed or timing a factor in our decision making?
Resourcing	What level of resourcing is required versus other options? How many projects could or should we take on at once?
Complexity	How complex is the development and implementation process, such as the number or types of partners, stakeholders and other interests?
Equity	Are there likely to be issues with equity, balance or cohesion in the partnerships that are required?

Criteria	Question to be asked
Commitment	Do all of our likely partners have enough at stake to drive a high level of commitment?
Timeframes	What are the timeframes and what milestones will show progress?
Portfolio	Does it fit in with the spread of opportunities, timelines and types of projects that we are seeking?
Risk	How does it rate in terms of implementation risk? What impact could it have on our reputation if it doesn't work?
Opportunity cost	Is there a potential cost and/or risk if we don't pursue this?

The potential value you can create needs to be assessed against a benchmark or yardstick to form a view about materiality. A small project with high potential may not materially improve the financial performance of your firm overall, despite having a significant impact within the division or cost centre supporting it. It is really up to you to determine what level of materiality you seek and create a policy or criteria to reflect that.

While it may be tempting to focus solely on the bigger breakthrough innovations, if you want to embed a culture of shared value across your business, I suggest disregarding size as long as it is attractive relative to the division or cost centre behind it. The larger projects make bigger contributions to your bottom line and the smaller ones help build the familiarity, skills and practices your people will need in systematically finding those larger opportunities. It's a question of how you want to build out your capability and what you want your portfolio of shared value inspired innovations to look like.

Whatever your preferred approach, well thought through criteria will guide you in the right direction. You may not have all the answers when you do your first screen – they can be firmed up as you build and iterate your business case – but if you find yourself making heroic assumptions or finding that the level of unknowns is high, there may be a good case for conducting further studies, trials or pilot programmes and developing prototypes before committing resources en masse, and we'll take these factors into account in the mapping process.

Mapping and iterating ideas

Once you have a strong concept and fair idea about the societal and business benefits you're trying to create, a good mapping process will help you identify who is doing what and why; it puts your own customers, social beneficiaries, key partners and stakeholders into focus and will help you identify the challenges to creating buy-in to your projects. It will also help you visualise success and the key risks or assumptions that need testing. Most of all, it will make your idea development process more efficient and effective. There's always a natural tension between too much detail and not enough so you'll need a format that is easy to use, accessible to many audiences, and one that supports rapid iterations.

The process described next is derived from a plan-on-a-page tool[98] designed in collaboration with design thinking expert Jane Cockburn and innovation guru Allan Ryan. There are five main elements as shown in Diagram 7.

Diagram 7: Mapping your ideas

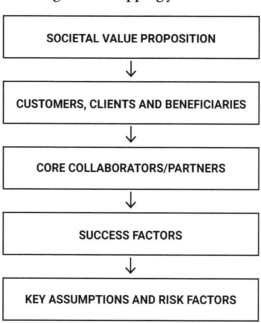

Note that if delivering societal outcomes is new to you or your team it's worth familiarising yourself with a methodology called "theory of change", which identifies the desired impacts and the specific actions required for achieving them. For now though, this mapping format will help fill the gap between your starting idea and your business case. Here are the key steps.

Step 1: Identify your "societal value proposition"

What is the positive social or environmental change that your idea is championing? Try and express it in a short sentence; then add three to five dot points explaining how it will work. In the Macarthur Real Estate Engagement Project, the societal value proposition is to reduce homelessness in Western Sydney. It will work by supporting tenants at risk, building trust between social services and the real estate sector, and creating access to opportunities for those in temporary housing, hostels or refuges. For Nestlé's Uncle Toby's Oats initiative, the societal value proposition is increasing the prosperity of the region by supporting crop diversification for farmers, and it will be achieved through research and development, tailored agronomy advice and flexible contracts that reduce delivery risk. Don't be surprised if your initial value proposition changes or morphs into something else as you tease out your idea. The value in defining your value proposition is that it anchors you and your fellow collaborators around a common goal.

Step 2: Customers, clients and beneficiaries

Who will benefit from your initiative? What problems are you solving or what opportunities are you creating for them? It may be broad, such as "rental property tenants in Western Sydney", or a tighter demographic such as "18-30-year-old single mothers renting in San Diego". Tenants at risk of eviction are the initial target demographic for the Western Sydney real estate initiative. However that project also has a longer term aim of building trust between agents and disadvantaged community members so that, in the future, there will be increased access to rental properties for people who are technically homeless. In other words, there may be more than one set of major beneficiaries. There may be other people, communities or organisations who aren't formally part of your project team but stand to benefit. The Battery World recycling initiative carried benefits for local government in the form of lower waste contamination, so it's important to identify everyone who is positively impacted by your actions.

Another worthy exercise is to frame the problem you are addressing in the language of your beneficiary. It's one thing to say the problem you are solving is "reducing unnecessary tenancy evictions", but they are not the words that an actual person in an at-risk situation would use. They may say "I've got so many hospital bills that I'm struggling to pay the rent." Going through this process helps you start building personas for your customer, client and beneficiary groups. When collaborating with project partners, the views or voice of the intended beneficiaries can, at times, get lost in amongst your own priorities. Building out personas helps bring focus when there are several project partners involved with anchoring questions like "How do you think Bill would feel in that situation?"

Step 3: Who are your core collaborators or partners?

List the partners whom you'll be *actively* working with to deliver the societal value proposition. If you have several similar organisations doing pretty much the same thing, such as local businesses or welfare providers, they can be listed together as a group. Keep your list focused on the significant and material contributors, and add stakeholders such as government agencies or regulators if they play a meaningful and active role.

You also want to express either the problem being solved or opportunity created for each of the parties you are collaborating with (including you) in the words they would use. If you can't easily identify the benefit for everyone involved that's a red flag. Engage further to try and work out what it is or accept that their ongoing participation may fall away if there is little value in it for them.

Step 4: Success factors

What are the key success factors for your initiative? What qualitative and quantitative indicators can you use to gauge success over the short, medium and longer terms, noting that you'll be potentially dealing with social, environmental, economic and financial variables.

We'll look more closely at measurement soon, but for now it might be helpful to imagine that you've gone overseas for three to five years and returned to find your project has magically been implemented and is successful – what indicators would tell you if it had worked or not? That's a good place to start and it might generate vigorous conversations between you and your colleagues. Your project partners may have different ideas about what constitutes success.

Measurement can be hard to get right, so don't get too bogged down by the practicality, cost or complexity of the actual measurement process. I'm confident you will find a reasonable way forward once you know exactly what you are aiming for. In Nestlé's Indian milk districts, the company finds it hard to calculate the total dollar value of the financial and economic benefits so it focuses on production volumes and average milk quality as proxy indicators[99]. Practicality over perfection will make your life easier. That's not to say there won't be situations where more detailed measurements are required, such as when government or not-for-profit partners have specific data or reporting needs.

Step 5: Key assumptions and risk factors

It hurts when a project falters or fails and someone says "I knew that would never work." Unearthing the elephant-in-the-room risks prior to going ahead is extremely valuable. The best questions to ask at this stage are: What are the main challenges that we know about? What could go wrong or pose an unacceptable risk? What assumptions are we making that need to be tested?

In our regional unemployment project in Wagga Wagga, people (mainly from outside the area) would often say that youths' inability to find a job must be due to an ice (methamphetamine) epidemic. However, having been on the ground and heard first-hand from residents, social service providers and the meat processing company, it turned out that, yes, there are some drug-related issues at play, although it's more likely to be marijuana than ice, but these issues usually represent the symptoms and not the cause; they are often the cumulative effects of problems that have gone before them. The point being that, in tackling the unemployment challenges in these regions, putting a lot of public or private sector resources into reducing ice use may be poorly targeted.

In the Battery World example where they put household battery drop-off bins in stores, there were two major risk factors: Firstly, if the margin on sales emanating from extra in-store foot traffic were lower than the battery collection and recycling costs, then the model would be financially unsustainable. Secondly, if the store licensee and/or their contracted recycling partner disposed of the batteries collected incorrectly (e.g. tipped them into the local creek) there would be a high risk of brand damage.

Risks can come in all shapes and sizes. Even basic risks like the turn-over of key staff can cause problems for any collaborative project, including shared value initiatives. This confirms yet again that they really should be treated like any other form of corporate project or partnership.

Building the business case

Your task is to create a business case and the format should be no different to the one you'd normally use. Having said that, some companies will consider tradeoffs or allowances in pursuing their shared value agenda. Reasons include the fact that they are dealing with a complex array of partners or development times are longer than usual; they may not have enough confidence to go ahead with a fully-fledged project without first running tests or trials; or they may be worried that their forecasts have too much room for error. Other forms of risk include poor relationships between project partners, resistance from the people impacted by change, consumers or business partners not responding as expected to new offerings or processes, insufficient training and so on. Some companies are more flexible in their rate of return requirements, accepting longer payback periods or lower hurdle rates of return. The parameters you use are up to you.

When confidence around an idea is low, government and foundation grants can play a 'catalytic' role (refer to Chapter 2), by helping to fund extra studies, pilot programmes or prototypes that increase the level of comfort before fully-fledged investments are made. As explained earlier, the Macarthur Real Estate Engagement Project was supported by a state government grant that allowed the peak body to develop its idea before proceeding to implementation. As a result, the participants had a greater level of comfort and risk was reduced by way of this grant funding.

For systemic change, industry bodies and forums are good engage-ment points due to their wide membership base. As Sue from Herbert Smith Freehills noted, the managing partners' forum was instrumental in bringing industry participants together to talk about diversification and inclusion issues and gave them the confidence they needed in positioning for change.

Overcoming internal challenges

Momentum is needed at all levels of your organisation to realise the full potential of shared value strategies. I found this out working in the investment industry, where fund managers are mainly differ-entiated by their key personnel, investment style and retrospective performance numbers. The firm I worked for saw an opportunity to create another source of differentiation by integrating the analysis of environmental, social and governance (ESG) risk factors (outlined in Chapter 2) into all of its investment decisions. We were a large firm so there was a relatively small cost in gaining the extra research resources we needed. Making investment decisions with more information rather than less seemed sensible and, over time, we expected it to translate into greater outperformance. We were also swimming with the tide, because our customers were coming to us wanting to know more about ESG analysis and how it could add value for them.

From an innovation perspective, this came out of an informal, internal militia (comprising three colleagues and myself) who were concerned about climate change as a global issue because we were starting to feel the impacts in our investment portfolios. For example, we had an exposure to a coal-fired power generation asset that, depending on the regulatory regime that prevailed, could be worth a little or a lot. We were partly blindsided by this risk, and there were tangible reasons for wanting to enhance our investment processes. At first we struggled in selling the idea upwards in our organisation; however with advent of the UN Principles for Responsible Investment championing the development of this type of analysis, senior management came on board. Much of our industry was taking a product-led approach by setting up ethical or socially responsible investment funds that would screen companies in or out according to a set of rules. In contrast, we wanted to make sure that a more detailed level of analysis would be mainstreamed across every investment in every portfolio, meaning that we'd be applying it across more than $140 billion of investments (stocks, bonds, property, infrastructure, etc.) rather than a handful of smaller funds with niche appeal.

The change management part of the project required us to engage with the heads of all of the investment units – they could opt in to the change if they wanted to. We found they weren't all enthusiastic about it. Some were incorrectly associating key phrases like "responsible investing" with ethical judgments and had shut themselves off to the idea of change even before the conversation began; or they thought we were there to tell them what they could and couldn't invest in. So the first phase consisted of many open and honest conversations, explaining that it was a means for enhancing investment processes, meeting the emerging needs of our customers and differentiating our brand. At the time we weren't aware of the shared value concept; however, in hindsight, our project was driven by the same principles. We wanted to allocate our investment capital better than our competitors by becoming skilled at assessing social and environmental factors. To develop the initiative we gained high-level support, aligned it with our strategic goals and were able to influence the majority of investment heads to come on board.

Multi-party project challenges

Collaborating across organisational boundaries is a skill set your people will need, requiring traits like curiosity, empathy and humility. The parties you're dealing with have their own motivations, work cultures and language. Unless you have external facilitation, the role of bringing together disparate groups will be a joint responsibility of all of the partners, although typically there will be one or two main drivers or process owners. From my own experiences in bringing multiple partners and stakeholders together, I've found it's worth finding the common speed that everyone can move at. Some partners will want to race ahead and get it all done in a hurry and others will be slow and steady, holding the course. Calibrate your development process to find the optimal speed that engages all of the key players.

Storytelling is important, and so is story listening. When we started scoping out our regional youth employment project in Wagga Wagga, we found trust was lacking because community members and representatives from social service providers held the meat processing business in poor regard. To paraphrase the conversations we were hearing, they saw the abattoir as "a pack of bastards who kill cows and employ [offshore] workers." The problem was that these views weren't consistent with reality. So, as part of the knowledge exchange and trust building process, we arranged for an employee of the company and local resident, Anthony, to tell his story at an event held at a local community centre. He told of how he'd been in prison for a time and soon after release his wife became pregnant. It shifted his thinking – he wanted to be a good father and get serious about earning money by getting a job. As a young Aboriginal man with a criminal record, finding a job wasn't easy, but the abattoir gave him a go. His first role was sweeping blood from the kill room floor. Anthony retained his positive attitude and strong work ethic and moved up through eight different positions over the next six years, including senior supervisory and quality assurance roles. Hearing his story helped fellow residents and social service providers realise that you can build a good career and lifestyle by working at an abattoir. This was a new and deeper form of engagement between the company and local community that helped us move forward. The fact that Anthony was a community member and employee of the company was certainly a strategic choice and helped create buy-in and trust.

Innovation also requires resilience. Your idea may run smoothly from concept to implementation, however it is more likely you'll have setbacks and challenges along the way. To illustrate the resilience challenge, in the same regional employment project we came across a young lady whom I'll call Trudy. She comes from a family where five successive generations have never held down a regular job. It's hard for those of us who've lived in working households to comprehend what that would be like and the extra challenges standing in her way. Growing up, she was rarely at school and had been in and out of the juvenile justice system. Trudy expressed interest in working at the abattoir, had an interview and was accepted. She completed the induction programme and enjoyed her first few days on the job. At this point our project team was feeling pretty good – a great social outcome and a promising development for the company in building out its workforce in new ways. Our joy lasted until the following Monday when Trudy didn't show up for work and it took several days to find out where she was. She was absent for two weeks and the company, to its credit, held her job open. When she was located, a fellow employee whom she knew and trusted went out of his way to provide transport to work and mentoring support. We became upbeat again when she came back and worked Monday, Tuesday and Wednesday. Then she quit on the Thursday. I'm sure her journey was not easy given the influences at play in her life.

Our project team was also having its highs and lows and, ultimately, we needed to unpack and learn from the experience – at times we wondered if it was ever going to work, if extra support could make a difference and many other questions. Thus the need for resilience. We were feeling a bit sorry for ourselves until it was pointed out that, for someone with Trudy's background, getting a job, completing induction and experiencing a week at work was a big step forward. As a postscript to her story, soon after quitting Trudy began volunteering at her local community centre to build up her hospitality skills, and as I was finalising the draft of this book I heard that she is now back out at the abattoir working full time. The process worked – it just took longer than expected. In isolation one job may not sound like a huge gain for the company, but it is all part of the process of breaking down the apprehensions the people in the community have about working there, and I suspect more people in Trudy's peer group will be inspired to follow her lead.

The groundwork and evidence we collected during our early investigations paid off, with a full-time coordinator now assigned to rolling the project out across all of the businesses in the area seeking entry-level workers. The coordinator's role is to focus on individual cases in order to find and fix process gaps in the pre- and post-employment processes and use this knowledge to create more robust, self-sustaining solutions. Approximately 40 jobs have been created in the first 15 months of the coordination process and nearly half of these are for youths identifying as Aboriginal. Businesses and not-for-profits are starting to collaborate, sometimes independently of the project process, which is a great indicator of mindset shift and systemic change.

Expected and unexpected opportunities

In that same project, as we did more exploring we uncovered new project partners who weren't on our initial radar screen. For example, the juvenile justice system wanted to find out if there was a way we could provide highly supervised work experience opportunities for the older kids in detention so that, upon release, they were more likely to walk straight into a job and less likely to get into trouble again[100]. A stronger pathway to employment could help them gain the confidence and independence they needed in breaking the detention cycle. Scoping out and developing partnerships like this is part of the coordinators' role.

Exploring with a shared value lens often leads to completely new or enhanced ideas – some anticipated and others out of the blue. Insights and knowledge will be valuable. In another exploration, Fuji Xerox Australia was seeking ways of creating a stream of younger skilled employees to support its growth[101]. It met with schools and not-for-profits to look into the reasons for kids in disadvantaged areas leaving school early. It turned out there were four main factors: literacy, wellbeing, teacher acumen and connections. The last factor was the one Fuji Xerox thought it could work on with suppliers by providing career pathways into the logistics industry. It had limited initial success, learning that scaling is a challenge and the business benefits were less tangible than hoped, but Fuji Xerox believes that the relationships built and understanding created with community partners will reveal opportunities over time.

Language and communications

If we can't understand each other we can't easily work together. They language we use is critical when working with people and organisations in other sectors and in complex projects and partnerships. Language in this context may refer to acronyms or jargon – to an accountant D&A could signify depreciation and amortisation, whereas to a social sector worker it could mean drugs and alcohol. The terms you use may not be well understood by all of your project partners and the role of project managers and facilitators includes translating conversations into a neutral language that everyone comprehends.

Language is also about the words and phrases you use to engage project partners. An example comes from the Macarthur Real Estate Engagement Project, which was struggling at one point because agents weren't grasping the commercial benefits of the opportunity. Eva's project team recruited a retired real estate agent to help improve the language they used. The objective of the project was originally described as "developing mutually beneficial relationships between real estate agents and services that work with the homeless and disadvantaged", and was subsequently modified to "we work with local real estate agents to reduce rent loss, introduce and sustain tenancies." It's only a subtle change; nevertheless it proved to be a powerful one.

Don't be afraid to describe and communicate business benefits when creating shared value. In a local government area in Melbourne we noticed that news articles about socially good actions tended to show business owners presenting larger-than-life cheques to charities; or there'd be work teams in whacky outfits doing charity fun runs or feel-good stories featuring disabled workers. These gave the impression that businesses should be charitable, which is not a problem; however when you are creating shared value you want to capture the business side of the narrative so that your own people and interested observers understand what's going on. We compiled summaries of several business and community initiatives that exhibited potential or actual shared value traits to show other companies in the area what was possible. This by-line from one of our case studies illustrates how the business benefit can be elevated:

> *"At Patterson Cheney Cars & Trucks, entry level training opportunities are not just about being a responsible business in the community, they also provide a source of good quality employees and contribute to its strong work culture"*

This dealership partnered with a job services provider to find disability-worker candidates with the right attributes for working in its car servicing centres, and found that by carefully selecting employees the outcomes for the business were as good, if not better, than sourcing trainees through normal recruitment channels. Across two dealership sites, Patterson Cheney has recruited 15 staff using this process, helping to create a strong staff culture, lower employee turnover, better customer service and, ultimately, improved financial performance. In our documented case study we made a conscious decision to spell out the benefits, namely that trainees have the opportunity to develop skills and create a pathway in areas suited to their capabilities, that the process has been integrated into business-as-usual for Patterson Cheney and its employment services partner, and that the company gains from a better quality of trainee than it is able to get through online advertising.

Sensitivity may also be needed in presenting business benefits. Despite the harsh findings of the recent banking inquiry in Australia, one of our big four banks, NAB, has a great example of shared value in action[102] where it is also wise to be careful and humble about how it is portrayed. The NAB Assist debt collections operation once had the highest complaint rate in the industry and it has worked hard to improve proactive support for customers in financial distress and make it easier for them to get back on their feet. Financial hardship can result from accidents, mental illness, gambling, substance abuse, homelessness or family violence. People awaiting decisions on claims for income protection or disability support payments are most at risk. NAB Assist includes coordinated access to mental health support services, and its frontline employees are equipped with Lifeline training to improve the way they interface with customers experiencing financial hardship. NAB also works closely with Kildonan UnitingCare to improve the way it handles vulnerable customers, ensuring that employees engage with empathy and respect.

In a recent report, the bank noted that, out of 18,000 customers facing financial difficulties throughout the year, 97 per cent were back on track within 90 days. Complaints to the ombudsman fell from 548 to 18 over a five-year period. From a commercial perspective, NAB estimates that it saves approximately $70 million per annum from proactively managing these hardship cases – representing the losses it would have incurred if a forced sale of secured assets had been required. Communicating commercial value needs to be done with care as it would be distasteful, especially in the context of the Royal Commission, to be boastful about making large profits from doing good, however we shouldn't shy away from the fact that financial incentive is what has brought greater resources to the problem and vastly improved outcomes for customers. What will NAB do with these extra savings? They could be applied in many ways, such as further investments in hardship prevention, funding a small reduction in lending rates to increase competitiveness or to boost profits. Communications need to be considered, thoughtful and respectful.

Measuring shared value

Recall there are two criteria: an economic benefit for the company in question coupled with a positive and measurable societal benefit. The criteria set out by Porter & Kramer is quite broad and there is no agreed methodology or approach to reporting on outcomes. A good measurement example comes from early studies[103] of cocoa farmers in Cote d'Ivoire, where improving smallholder farmer yields raised incomes by more than 300 per cent. My overarching advice is to approach measurement as if you were communicating the key economic, social and environmental indicators to your management, key partners and stakeholders. It's less about public relations and more about knowing whether your internal resources are being well allocated. The level of depth you go into is really your choice. Your main challenge is to produce indicators that provide evidence of a link between your initiative and the benefits created.

Reflecting on the social side of the equation, you will need to delineate between inputs, activities, outputs, outcomes and impacts. I'm sure that sounds like a lot of variables to consider but it is for good reason. Inputs are the resources such as funding, equipment and volunteers used in project implementation. Activities are what you do in executing the plan, such as adapting policies, developing procedures or conducting meetings and information sessions. Outputs refer to immediate, direct indicators (the number of meetings held, the percentage of people who sign up for a programme). Outcomes typically reflect what has changed in the medium term as a result of the plan being executed (the number of jobs attained, decrease in staff turnover) and impacts are the long-term consequences of the project

151

(such as youths breaking the cycle of unemployment and improved workforce productivity).

Sam Moore, former Head of Shared Value at Bendigo and Adelaide Bank, concluded[104] that "there's not a simple yes/no answer to the question of whether a strategy is or isn't shared value. It's more helpful to ask to what extent a strategy is reflective of shared value principles". Porter & Kramer note[105] that the tools to put this concept into practice are still in their infancy and companies lack the data they need to optimise results. A review of the existing guidance on measurement[106] compiled by fellow practitioner Andrew Hamilton and myself is recommended as further reading. Don't ignore measurement but, at the same time, don't let the intricacies of measurement hold you back. Proxy indicators can usually be found that will provide solid evidence of the change you are seeking to create.

Monitoring, learning and refining

Once you've developed your idea further, created a business case and gained approval for implementation, there's the monitoring, review and refinement process to deal with. Steering groups with broad representation help you deal with project challenges and identify extra opportunities that come up along the way. I can't emphasise enough how much insight you will gain as you progress. We saw it with Fuji Xerox Australia, where its employment prototype wasn't as successful as hoped for; however it gave great insights into what Fuji Xerox needed to do in terms of refinement. And in our regional employment challenge in Wagga Wagga we came across new types of partners who weren't initially on our radar, and the evidence we collected in that exploration phase led to it being scaled up from one business to include all businesses in the region seeking entry-level workers.

Innovation is hard; and innovation using a shared value lens is even harder. There's no rule that says you have to do it one way or the other. The processes outlined in this section will help you bridge the gap between an appreciation of the principles and creating action, and I expect you will figure out what works for you as you try things out. You stand to reap great rewards if you are successful.

SECTION IV

your
action
plan

The ideas in this book may be new to you, or they may be formalising your intuitive thoughts or existing actions. Whatever your background or skill in this area, it only has meaning if you do something with it; and that could be a very simple first step – it doesn't need to be a convoluted project or complex strategy. This final section gives you a chance to take stock, do a quick review and figure out what you do from here.

chapter 12
taking the next step

We are all in this together. What goes on in society affects company performance, and corporate activities impact our lives. Shared value is a tangible and powerful concept for bridging profit and purpose, creating a better future through everyday business.

The way we do business is changing

We've looked at the competing interests between business and society and how, traditionally, corporations have relied upon their philanthropic and CSR agendas to make a difference. They do make a difference, but not at the scale necessary to drive meaningful change. Walmart's Chief Sustainability Officer, Kathleen McLaughlin, summed it up well[107] when she noted that Walmart no longer has a notion of philanthropy or CSR as being separate undertakings; it looks to the business itself to create value and strengthen the systems it relies on in society.

Shared value is merely a new lens that companies can use to inno-vate and generate sustained profits; however it's a very effective one because it builds trust and creates positive impacts at the same time. As we've seen, leading corporations are putting it into practice and getting the edge on their competitors, or working collaboratively to lift the performance of entire industries or regions. They understand that corporate purpose is no longer a decorative feature: it is a strategic weapon in their arsenal.

To quote a well-worn saying, the only constant in business these days is change. Social norms today aren't what they were yesterday. When I look back at my family's association with the Cadbury brand, social attitudes and standards continue to evolve. My grandmother, Winifred Frappell, who was the daughter of great-grandfather George Frappell, worked at the Cadbury factory in Hobart and met her husband-to-be at a company social function. The policy at the time was for women to resign once they married, and she did. That clearly is not acceptable today, although some companies do require one partner of a married couple to resign and seek employment elsewhere.

The way customers feel about your products and services, your brands and the way you do business is changing all the time. Employees expect to be treated well, and the best talent in the market is looking for something special in the organisations they choose to work for. Social trends influence the rules and regulations in your industry and the motivation for activists to take aim at you. With higher standards of living come higher expectations, and it's much harder to hide harmful or suboptimal practices in an age of media democratisation.

Anticipating and keeping up with change is challenging. It also provides the opportunity to evolve in a way that feels right for the times, where you can deliver profit and purpose in lock-step with each other as reinforcing rather than competing interests. The shared value concept provides the means for unlocking that value, and I'm confident it will be integral to the corporate success stories of the future as well as being the key to addressing the great challenges of our time.

Overall, shared value requires the right win-win mindset and supporting skills. The aim of this book is to explain the shared value concept and equip you with the methods and tools for putting it into action. It's over to you now.

What insights have you gained? What resonates with you? What is your plan from here?

What does success look like?

If there were to be one solid indicator that we as a society have grasped this way of thinking, it would be when a company announces a strategy that has shared value characteristics and stock market analysts are willing and able to ascribe value to it immediately instead of waiting for the months or years it takes for the dollars to flow through to the bottom line. It's a world where our capital – financial, human, social, ecological and economic – is allocated in the best possible way, with mutual gain front of mind for everyone. That's the point where we'll know we are all working in each other's interests and we're in good hands.

What would your ideal business look like? What new activities would be going on? What different types of conversations would be heard in your boardroom? How could you glean greater insights from your front-line staff? Whom might you be partnering with tomorrow that you're not partnering with today?

I trust this book has helped you appreciate, reinvigorate or enhance the role you can play in the future, and inspired you to make it happen.

You get to decide

At a personal level, how good would it feel to have a seamless blend between your day job and making a difference? I know from personal experience that it's tempting to set a goal of making lots of money so that you can give something back later in life. Along the way I realised I didn't want to wait that long, that many issues I wanted to address couldn't wait that long, nor did I want my actions to be token or lacking in significance.

I had a feeling that there had to be a better way of doing business, but struggled to articulate what it could be and how to get executives and shareholders to buy in or care about it. The good news is that we now have a language and set of principles to describe the solution. We don't need to abandon capitalism in search of another way; the profit motive is one of the best levers we have in creating change. It's about changing the way we use capitalism so that it plays to our collective advantage.

We can build a future that is good for us, our families, the communities we live in and the planet we inhabit.

Connecting profit with purpose

There's one action that matters: your first one. What is the one thing you can do today or tomorrow as a result of this? It may be as simple as introducing the topic into a daily meeting, adding it to your board agenda or examining the challenges your business faces using a shared value framework to eke out new opportunities.

This isn't about reconfiguring your business; it is about enhancing it, adding an extra lens to your existing practices. Over time your ideas will grow and evolve – perhaps you'll even review your corporate purpose in light of this conversation. Get traction by laying the groundwork now.

If you work in government, I'd urge you to add a shared value lens to improve the way industry can help solve your problems – where you become co-designers of solutions. And likewise for not-for-profits: you and industry need each other if you are both to succeed.

As you shape your ideas, keep in mind some will grow and others will peter out. Some will start out in a certain direction and change course as new insights are uncovered. That's normal. The challenge lies in having the courage and means to move forward.

You can connect profit with purpose and create a world-changing business.

acknowledgements

The ideas and process of getting this book together took some time, and I have to say that I first and foremost have to thank Karen for encouraging my own personal growth and supporting my journey to a new vocation from late 2007 onwards – little did either of us know about the financial insecurity that comes with such a radical change in career! She's put up with my hours in the study that seem to vacuum up time. And to Hannah and Joel, who likely missed out on some Dad time here and there because of it. Unfortunately my mother, Judy, after a long and debilitating illness, didn't see the end result; however my father, Ian, has. The sentiment of the book – that we can all get on just fine if we put our minds to it – is one that they've both championed all their lives, along with a strong belief in fairness, hard work and respect for each other. So I thank them with all my heart for what they instilled in us. And I'd like to thank sister Lyn for the central role she plays in maintaining our family unit while her younger sibling is living elsewhere and writing books. It's sad that our brother, Scott, succumbed to an illness several years ago.

I refer to Paul Gilding (author of *The Great Disruption*) in the footnotes. He helped shape my own thoughts about more proactive approaches to advancing business and society as a whole. Another significant figure is Jenny Briscoe-Hough, whose soul and wisdom shine so brightly that early on in my journey every conversation seemed to be a lesson in becoming a greater human being. Allan Ryan and Jane Cockburn have been instrumental in their innovation and design experience, as applying shared value concepts often requires us to be across many disciplines at once.

For articulating the shared value concept that formalises the link between profit with purpose, thanks must of course go to Professor Michael Porter and the ever encouraging Mark Kramer. My life is infinitely richer for being able to work with such a wide range of organisations on important challenges – a far cry from what a mathematics major turned investment research manager would have thought he'd ever be doing. A quick mention of some of my closer acquaintances who have been championing the shared value concept: Helen Steel, Rhod Ellis-Jones and Andrew Hamilton.

Out in the field, some of the significant projects that I've been able to assist with in regional New South Wales are referred to in the book. Donna Argus deserves a special shout out for her tireless, great work in Wagga Wagga – work that I suspect is underappreciated in the whole scheme of things – and Gerry Collins who proved a great partner for our travails in Bourke. I also value the opportunity to have delivered shared value education internally to IAG over several years and witnessed its courage in taking the road less travelled. Further mentions must go out to Carole Ferguson for lively lunchtime catch-ups and the support she's provided in my career U-turn, to Kyrn Stevens for the exploratory work we did in the top end of Australia, and to Eva Gerencer who led the real estate agents' engagement efforts and allowed me to capture the case study with her. Likewise, Greg Leslie at Battery World Townsville from Helen Lewis' introduction and to Edwina Beveridge of Blantyre Farms with an introduction from Jeremy Hutchings.

Professional support in the production of the book itself has come from my wonderful book coach Jaqui Lane and draft reviewers Michael O'Byrne, Ross Clennett, Rebecca Fry, Elliott Bowen, Scott Machin, James Young, Andrew Hamilton and Lawrence Wray. Apart from encouragement, they picked up some significant areas for improvement that have made a lot of difference to the end product. Former colleagues Tony Adams, Tony FitzGerald and Warren Bird have been regular accomplices in discussing financial market implications.

For my peer support team, including Neryl, Peter, Danielle, John, Thomas and Steven, our catch ups are the highlight of my month and provide much of the re-energising that's needed to keep soldiering on. Another peer support network has been the book club I have belonged to for the past 10 years – Peter, Alex, Tom, Woody and Vernon – we've taken on some significant texts including the writings of Robert Tressell and his *Ragged-Trousered Philanthropists*, so thanks for the extended learning and philosophical (and sometimes not-so-philosophical) debates.

Thanks all.

challenging the concept

A powerful concept should be able to withstand an open and candid discussion about its benefits and limitations. Here are answers to questions that commonly arise:

1. How does shared value help build trust in business and capitalism?

Falling levels of consumer trust have led to calls to fix capitalism and for companies to be 'good'. The concept is valid and strong, however creating a consensus definition of what is good is problematic, so the boundaries are not always clear nor agreed upon. Changing or abandoning the shareholder profit motive would be a monumental shift away from the current system and we'd be struggling to work out what to replace it with, let alone agree on it. Shared value is about learning how to be smarter within our current system.

The advantage of shared value is that it is practical and provides a bridge between profit and purpose. It is an enhancement, not an ideological change. It won't solve every societal problem we have because it's only effective when there's an overlap between the business agenda and a societal issue but, when it does work, it can create greater impact for longer compared to philanthropy and CSR. BlackRock's Larry Fink made the point[108] to his investor clients that companies cannot solve all issues of importance, but there are many issues that cannot be solved without corporate leadership.

2. What are the critics saying?

The concept hasn't always been favourably received because Porter & Kramer highlighted the shortcomings of CSR in their earlier papers, which provoked a strong response from academics and practitioners. The main criticism came in a paper[109] by Crane, Palazzo, Spence & Matten. In my view, they have interpreted shared value as a competing practice to CSR, whereas they are in fact complementary. They suggest that shared value proponents want to sideline ethics and social norms, which means they are confusing a lens for corporate innovation with the fundamentals of good management and administration. There is no reason why companies could or should apply different standards when creating shared value. And they imply that the advocates of shared value believe it will rectify capitalism. As I've noted, it isn't a magic cure for everything; however it provides a roadmap for companies to address genuine societal needs and that can only be good in the long run. As we saw from the examples of JP Morgan Chase & Co, IAG and Pearson, substantial companies are taking purpose very seriously. Notwithstanding disagreements with some of their key points, I am in agreement with the authors' summation that collective and collaborative methods are required to address our biggest challenges, and that shared value is a pathway for increasing company engagement.

3. When is shared value most effective?

Shared value works at the intersection of meaningful corporate challenges or market needs and societal problems. This means that there are also many problems where shared value will play little or no role, and that CSR agendas, foundation grants, government grants, commissioned interventions, policy levers and other means will still be needed. A shift that I think has been underestimated through the introduction of shared value terminology is that it has helped companies engage with a broader set of stakeholders and partners.

4. Has it ever led to poor social trade-offs or covering up bad business?

Sometimes, yes. Shared value has become a new, trendy concept for the corporate world and some claims don't stand up to scrutiny. There is no formal control over the use of the term, which can lead to "shared value-washing" – perhaps the next iteration of green-washing.

Take, for example, the tobacco company celebrating a sustainable packaging award. It's hard to ignore the profound health impacts associated with its core products. Or Ben & Jerry's, the subsidiary of Unilever that's a celebrated brand for its social remit and B-Corp status, and yet it sells products high in sugars and fat. Or Australian banks like the NAB that have been exposed for illegal and unconscionable practices but have achieved great things in their debt collections area. Such a mix of positive social impacts and externalities must be challenging for an ethical purist. There are not always easy, clear-cut answers, but it's better to probe and engage rather than avoiding them altogether.

It's also worth pointing out that, as Cadbury was being praised for looking after its employees, claims emerged in 1909 about the use of slave labour in the Portuguese colony of Sao Tome, the world's largest cocoa exporter at the time. To Cadbury's credit, this led to establishing new cocoa sources and supply chain practices to quell the adverse publicity.

5. Is it acceptable to profit from addressing societal challenges?

In the examples we've looked at, the companies in question wouldn't have had the resources to persist if they weren't growing their bottom line. Their CSR budgets would have barely scratched the surface of the problems they took on. Profit and purpose don't have to go head to head; they can go hand in hand.

Successfully linking financial and societal goals creates a reinforcing loop, one that is less likely to fall away when business conditions are challenging or there's turnover in senior management. Many not-for-profits are enthusiastically participating in shared value dialogue because of the far greater impact they can make. Recall that former President of the Rockefeller Foundation Judith Rodin pointed out (Chapter 2) that making real headway on social issues relies on gaining access to, and making better use of, private sector resources.

I doubt Cisco would have spent hundreds of millions of dollars partnering with public institutions to provide online curricula, teacher training and professional development for instructors if it wasn't seeking to improve some aspect of business, namely the quality of skills in the labour market that it relies upon for future growth.

6. Is this a way for Western companies to legitimise their developing market activities?

Multinational companies are utilising shared value principles to grow their businesses in developing countries. Take the coalition of companies mobilised by Mars providing assistance to help small-holder farmers in Cote d'Ivoire improve their cocoa crop quality and yields[110]. The country accounts for 40 per cent of world cocoa production and companies like Mars have a vested interest in supporting them due to the rising global demand for chocolate products.

Today, the Cadbury brand is part of the Mondelez empire and has a US$400 million global programme[111] underway to address looming cocoa shortages. Its work across several countries, such as India, Indonesia, Cote d'Ivoire, Brazil and the Dominican Republic is based on a model developed in Ghana where investments are made at a community level. The three main focus areas are promoting cocoa farming as a business opportunity and not just subsistence farming, empowering community members and conserving forests. Partnerships with organisations such as World Vision bring community development skills and greater levels of trust to the programme.

Forming a project using shared value principles may indeed create legitimacy for the good reason that the investments are producing mutual gains. This provides a template for breaking away from a model of selling to one of listening, evaluating and co-creating. It's not so good if the creation of shared value by a company is being touted widely and at the same time masking usurious behaviour in other parts of its business. That should be called out and challenged.

Weighing up competing social impacts is the main challenge corporations need to address. A mining company operating in Africa helped fund a highway upgrade to one of its project sites. As a result, there were economic benefits that came with improved infrastructure. On the flip side, a township bypassed by the new road lost its passing trade. The question for companies is: do they understand the associated negative impacts? Are they willing to include reasonable levels of mitigation into their business case? Are they willing to be transparent about those impacts?

7. Does every social initiative need to exhibit shared value?

Definitely not. We've already noted that corporate philanthropy and CSR initiatives do play a role – some of them may become pathways into shared value strategies as insights and hands-on experience are gained. Many Australian companies have developed Reconciliation Action Plans that could, for example, include scholarships or work placements for indigenous students. Offering five scholarships across a workforce of 5,000 is a relatively low impact activity and would be considered as CSR, however that does provide the company with new insights that could lead to more exciting innovations down the track. In fact, consulting firm PwC Australia supported the creation of an indigenous partner-led consulting business[112]. To do so, it deviated from its standard requirement of holding a majority ownership stake in such businesses in order for the founding partners to have control, a factor deemed critical for its success.

Moving forward together

When reading critiques or fielding tough questions about shared value, I sense that we all want the same outcome: economic and social prosperity. The main problem to overcome is that we see different paths for getting there. I'd encourage you to seek out and read reviews and critiques of the concept, all the while keeping in mind it is a set of principles for corporate innovation.

endnotes

1   Fortune's Change the World List 2017 can be found at
    https://fortune.com/change-the-world/2017/search/
    accessed Nov 10, 2019

2   By Canadian based research firm, Corporate Knights,
    that produces rankings and ratings based on corporate
    sustainability performance. The 2019 list can be found
    at https://www.corporateknights.com/reports/2019-
    global-100/2019-global-100-results-15481153/
    accessed Nov 10, 2019

3   United Nations Department of Economic and Social Affairs,
    Population Division

4   Earth Overshoot Day calculation based on Global Footprint
    Network data, found on https://www.footprintnetwork.org/

5   The European Commission adopted a strategy of adaptation
    to climate change in 2013

6   For an excellent text outlining how this will play out refer, Paul
    Gilding, *The Great Disruption* (Bloomsbury Publishing, 2011)

7   The not-for-profit entity, *Australian Packaging Covenant Organisation*, is tasked with coordinating and delivering these goals

8   According to Australia's national science research agency, CSIRO, *State of the Climate 2018* report

9   Australian Financial Review, *Lloyd's Neal on climate, Brexit, sex* (Nov 4, 2019)

10   McKinsey & Company, *Getting organizational redesign right* (McKinsey Quarterly, June 2015)

11   Buffett & Eimicke, *How Companies, Governments, and Nonprofits Can Create Social Change Together* (HBR 2018)

12   DDI, *Global Leadership Forecast 2018*

13   Sourced from jfklibrary.org

14   The Social Progress Imperative is a US not-for-profit entity aiming to complement economic measures with social and environmental data to prioritise actions that accelerate social progress

15   More about these and other historical examples can be found in, John Browne, *Connect* (WH Allen 2016)

16   As described in a blog by Howard Lake https://fundraising. co.uk/2008/09/15/lehman-brothers039-charitable-activities/ accessed Nov 10, 2019

17   The 2018 Edelman Trust Barometer

18   The New York Times, *How We've Reported on the Secrets and Power of McKinsey & Company* (Feb 19, 2019)

19   Martin Wolf, *We must rethink the purpose of the corporation*, (Financial Times, Dec 12, 2018)

20   Milton Friedman, *The Social Responsibility Of Business Is To Increase Its Profits*, (The New York Times Magazine, Sep 13, 1970)

21   The Business Roundtable statement, *Business Roundtable Redefines the Purpose of a Corporation to Promote 'An Economy That Serves All Americans'*, (Aug 19, 2019)

22   For more information refer https://www.netacad.com/

23   Porter & Kramer, *Creating Shared Value* (Harvard Business Review, Jan-Feb 2011)

24   Bloomberg, *Here's a Good Reason to End Quarterly Guidance: It Doesn't Work* (Jun 8, 2018)

25   Various sources including: *Interface & Volans, Interface the Untold Story of Mission Zero in Europe* (2014)

26   The New York Times, *McKinsey Advised Purdue Pharma How to 'Turbocharge' Opioid Sales, Lawsuit Says* (Feb 1, 2019)

27   The New York Times, *Museums Cut Ties With Sacklers as Outrage Over Opioid Crisis Grows* (Mar 25, 2019)

28   The New York Times, *Purdue Pharma, Maker of OxyContin, Files for Bankruptcy* (Sep 15, 2019)

29   Comments made at the Shared Value Leadership Summit in New York (May 2014)

30   FSG blog, *What is Catalytic Philanthropy* (Nov 4, 2015)

31   Sources include L M McDonald, *Corporate Social Responsibility (CSR) in banking: what we know, what we don't know, and what we should know* (2015)

32   Investopedia, *The 3 Pillars of Corporate Sustainability* (Updated Jun 16, 2019)

33   Sourced from Kimberly-Clark's website, https://www.
      sustainability2022.com/ accessed Nov 4, 2019

34   John Elkington, *25 Years Ago I Coined the Phrase "Triple Bottom
      Line." Here's Why It's Time to Rethink It* (Harvard Business
      Review, Jun 25, 2018)

35   Such as Danish pharmaceutical company, Novo Nordisk, the
      Anglo-Dutch Unilever and Germany's Covestro

36   BlackRock's *Annual Letter to CEOs* (Jan 15, 2020)

37   Australian Financial Review, *Facing carmageddon, RACQ says
      Millennials provide mutual hope* (Jul 22, 2019)

38   More information on https://bcorporation.net/

39   More information can be found on http://logantogether.org.au/

40   Fukuyama, F (1995), *Trust: The Social Virtues and The Creation
      of Prosperity*, Free Press, New York

41   Deloitte. Insights, *The rise of the social enterprise: 2018 Deloitte
      Global Human Capital Trends*

42   Australian Stock Exchange data, accessed Nov 1, 2019

43   As reported on https://www.bendigobank.com.au/community/
      community-bank accessed Nov 1, 2019 along with various
      other company sources

44   Shared Value Project Case Study: *Shared Value in Banking:
      The Community Bank Model*, by Sam Moore (undated)

45   As stated on https://www.bendigoadelaide.com.au/in_the_
      community/index.asp accessed Nov 6, 2019

46   Booklet, *Australian Packaging Covenant Awards Night:
      Celebrating the Achievement of Innovative High Performing APC
      Signatories* (2014)

47 For example, refer Straub, R, *What Management Needs to Become in an Era of Ecosystems*, (Harvard Business Review Jun 5, 2019)

48 Ibid. 29

49 Sourced from the 2017 annual report

50 City A.M., *Pearson shares sink as print woes hurt 2020 profit target* (Jan 16, 2020)

51 John Browne, *Connect* (WH Allen 2016), pp 22-27

52 Comments made at the Share Value Summit (2019) in Sydney, Australia

53 FSG guide entitled, *Creating Shared Value: A How-to Guide for the New Corporate (R)evolution*, sponsored by HP and authored by Bockstette & Stamp

54 Meier & Cassar, *Stop Talking About How CSR Helps Your Bottom Line* (Harvard Business Review, Jan 31, 2018)

55 Based on Fortune's Global 500 analysis (2019), where revenues were US$32.7 trillion and profits US$2.15 trillion

56 Gerard Teliis, *Toyota's gamble on the Prius* (Financial Times Mar 5, 2013)

57 Ibid. 46

58 Ibid. 23

59 Comments made by Gary Cohen at the Share Value Summit (2019) in Sydney, Australia

60 Sourced from Nestlé Oceania's *Creating Shared Value Report 2009* and Shared Value Initiative case study, *Uncle Tobys – Sustainable Oat Production in Rural Australia*, by Melinda Leth (undated)

61 Refer https://www.iag.com.au/about-us/who-we-are/purpose-and-strategy accessed Nov 7, 2019

62 Background can be found at http://iag.com.au/node/1916 accessed Nov 7, 2019

63 According to various reports issued by the *Australian Business Roundtable for Disaster Resilience & Safer Communities* found on http://australianbusinessroundtable.com.au/

64 From panel discussion featuring local managing directors at the Australian Food & Grocery Council Future Leaders Forum 2018 held in Sydney, Australia

65 As outlined on https://www.herbertsmithfreehills.com/diversity-and-inclusion accessed Nov 7, 2019

66 Shared Value Initiative case study, *CJ Korea Express: Senior Parcel Delivery* (undated, no author name)

67 Shared Value Project case study, *Blantyre Farms – Re-purposing Food Waste to Boost Farm and Manufacturer Profitability*, by Phil Preston & Jeremy Hutchings (undated)

68 Shared Value Initiative case study, *Enel: Redefining the Value Chain* (Dec 2016)

69 For further information, refer https://sharedvalue.org.au/shared-value-leader-enel-starts-production-australia/ accessed Nov 7, 2019

70 Kramer & Pfitzer, *The Ecosystem of Shared Value* (Harvard Business Review, Oct 2016)

71 Roy Morgan's *Image of Professions Survey 2017*

72 Shared Value Initiative case study, *Reducing Homelessness Through Commercial Incentive for Real Estate Agents*, by Gerencer & Preston (2015)

73 Ibid. 23

74 Such as *The Truth About CSR* by Rangan et al (Harvard Business Review 2015) or Besharov et al, *How Companies Can Balance Social Impact and Financial Goals* (Harvard Business Review 2019)

75 Shared Value Project case study, *Suncorp Group & Good Shepherd Microfinance*, by Desmond Lim (undated), and various other articles

76 ABC News, *Hole in the ozone layer is finally 'healing'* (Jul 1, 2016)

77 Interview with Matthew Quinn along with the Shared Value Project case study snapshot, *Stockland: Creating liveable communities through shared value*, by Leth, Hems & Turner (undated)

78 First position in Fortune's Change the World List 2017

79 More project information can be found at https://investdetroit.com/

80 As described in https://www.jpmorganchase.com/corporate/news/pr/jpmc-launches-500mm-advancingcities-initiative.htm accessed Nov 9, 2019

81 Referencing https://sustainability.lionco.com/lion-receives-shared-value-project-award/ accessed Nov 9, 2019

82 Shared Value Project interview with Libby Davidson, https://sharedvalue.org.au/shared-value-champions-libby-davidson/ accessed Nov 9, 2019

83 LinkedIn posting by Libby Davidson, https://www.linkedin.com/pulse/creating-shared-value-lion-libby-davidson/ accessed Nov 9, 2019

84 As stated on Lion's website, https://www.lionco.com/about-us/
our-vision-and-purpose accessed Nov 9, 2019

85 Shared Value Initiative case study, *Patrimonio Hoy: Access to
Housing and Finance* (undated)

86 Shared Value Initiative case study: *Anadarko: Staying Ahead of
the Curve in Mozambique*, by Katie Levy (undated)

87 Australian Financial Review, *Life insurer AIA Australia wants
action big and small on mental health* (Apr 11, 2018)

88 Shared Value Initiative case study, *BD: Healthcare Worker Safety*
(undated)

89 Pfitzer, Bockstette & Stamp, *Innovating for Shared Value*
(Harvard Business Review, Sep 2013)

90 Osterwalder & Pigneur, *Business Model Generation: A
Handbook for Visionaries, Game Changers, and Challengers*
(John Wiley & Sons, Jul 13, 2010)

91 ABC Background Briefing investigation by Alex Mann,
*Not fare: How taxi licences collapsed in value, destroying lives and
livelihoods* (Aug 5, 2018)

92 Refer https://www.un.org/sustainabledevelopment/
sustainable-development-goals/

93 Shared Value Initiative case study: *Creating Sustained
Competitive Advantage*, by Phil Preston (undated)

94 Malnight, Buche & Dhanaraj, *Put Purpose at the Core of Your
Strategy* (Harvard Business Review, Sep-Oct 2019)

95 Comments made at the Share Value Summit (2018) in Sydney,
Australia

96   Chevreux, Lopez & Mesnard, *The best companies know how to balance strategy and purpose* (Harvard Business Review, Nov 2, 2017)

97   Article by John Batelle, https://shift.newco.co/2017/04/05/business-exists-to-serve-society/ accessed Nov 10, 2019

98   For more information, contact the author via phil@philpreston.com.au

99   FSG guide authored by Porter et al, *Measuring Shared Value: How to Unlock Value by Linking Social and Business Results*

100 Disturbingly, it turns out that there are some kids who deliberately commit crimes in order to get into the juvenile justice system because life is more structured and ordered on the inside compared to problems and uncertainties they face at home.

101 As reported on http://www.probonoaustralia.com.au/news/2013/12/creating-shared-value-practical-lessons-future accessed Nov 10, 2019

102 Sources include: NAB Dig Deeper Report 2016, NAB 2018 Sustainability Report and Shared Value Project profile of Sasha Courville (Apr 1, 2016)

103 Ibid. 23

104 From the resource, *Shared Value Measurement*, by Andrew Hamilton & Phil Preston that can be found on http://sharedvalue.org.au/wp-content/uploads/2018/06/SV-Measurement-Resource-Hamilton-Preston-18-06-04.pdf

105 FSG guide authored by Porter et al, *Measuring Shared Value: How to Unlock Value by Linking Social and Business Results*

106 Ibid. 104

107 Article by John Batelle, https://shift.newco.co/2017/04/05/ business-exists-to-serve-society/ accessed Nov 10, 2019

108 BlackRock's 2019, *Letter to CEOs*, can be found at https://www.blackrock.com/corporate/investor-relations/ larry-fink-ceo-letter

109 Crane, Palazzo, Spence & Matten, *Contesting the Value of "Creating Shared Value"* (California Management Review, Vol 56, No. 2, Winter 2014)

110 Ibid. 89

111 As outlined on https://www.cocoalife.org/the-program/ approach accessed Nov 10, 2019

112 This business is outlined on https://www.pwc.com.au/ indigenous-consulting.html accessed Nov 10, 2019

Index

Tables and diagrams

notes

notes

notes

notes

notes

about the author

When Phil Preston left his corporate career to explore the challenges faced by grassroots community members and not-for-profits, he found an astonishing level of disconnection between business and society.

He also noticed that philanthropy and corporate social responsibility initiatives have limited impact, so when he stumbled across Michael Porter and Mark Kramer's 'shared value' concept he went all in. In 2013 he was invited to Boston to help form a network of global practitioners, and subsequently increased his focus on harnessing the power of business for positive societal change.

Phil is a strategist, facilitator and speaker who resides south of Sydney with his wife, adult children and manic dog, Gizmo. He is an enthusiastic trail runner in his spare time.

Website: philpreston.com.au
Email: phil@philpreston.com.au
Phone: +61 408 259 633

To order further copies of the book please make contact via :

orders@philpreston.com.au

Note that discounts are available for bulk orders.

Lightning Source UK Ltd.
Milton Keynes UK
UKHW030713111022
410294UK00015B/738